Good Guns
Again

A Celebration of Fine Sporting Arms

Stephen J. Bodio

Good Guns *Again*

A Celebration of Fine Sporting Arms

by

Stephen J. Bodio

Illustrated by
Christopher S. Smith

Wilderness Adventures Press™
Bozeman, Montana

Dedication

So close a friend
      as this
a man cannot trade
for five pony loads
      of silver
or ten young maidens.

      -Thai (Laku) hunter
      (of his ancient muzzle-
        loading rifle)

      - suggested by Father Anderson
      Bakewell, S.J.

Good Guns *Again*

A Celebration of Fine Sporting Arms

Stephen J. Bodio

Foreword

You are reading this book for one of two reasons: Either you like good guns, or you like Steve Bodio. Maybe both. And that's understandable, because it's easy to like both.

Known for years for his penetrating book reviews in *Gray's Sporting Journal*, Steve originally wrote *Good Guns* in 1986. At that time, he didn't consider it complete. Much has happened to the author and to the gun trade since then, the author, the trade — and the book — being works-in-progress.

This book looks at Bodio's opinions and experiences in a lifetime of thrashing about accumulating guns he likes and isn't ashamed to trot out in public. That he happens to be one of the finest writers in the English-speaking world on this or any other topic is a bonus. You are going to find out for yourself about the book; I'd like to tell you a bit about Bodio.

The label "Renaissance Man" could aptly be stuck on this transplanted New Englander. He enjoys good art, falconry, about any kind of wine he can manage to get the cork out of, and is a voracious reader of fine literature. He commutes between his home in Magdalena, New Mexico and the haunts of a few close friends in Bozeman, Montana. I can tell you for a fact that he is a tireless hunter, crack shot, and bottomless well of tales, opinions, and reflections. I also consider him a close friend.

He likes any good gun, short English shells, sour mash whiskey, and his springer spaniel, Bart.

If you've ever met Steve through his writing before, you know what to expect; if this is your first time, get ready for a treat.

Steve Smith
Traverse City, Michigan

Acknowledgements

You cannot make a book without help from your friends. My father came first. By his example, I learned about nature, birdwatching, hunting and safety, competence, and aesthetics as though they were all parts of one subject. I first learned about good guns from him, and his perfectionism will always be a part of me. The late Betsy Huntington put up with and even abetted my maniacal acquisition of guns (and books and animals) for years, sharing my enthusiasm, but tempering my wilder swings with her Yankee practicality. Her influence has probably made it a bit easier for my partner today, Libby Frishman, who continues to indulge me.

I stand on the shoulders of many writers, living and dead. Ones that have written to answer my incessant questions include the late Roger Barlow, Geoffrey Boothroyd, Bob Brister, John Hill, Douglas S.A. McDougall, Ross Seyfried, Eric Swann, and Bill Wise; David Simpson, Texas renaissance man and good-gun fanatic, whose fields include art, writing, stockmaking, and stream biology, has exchanged a small book's worth of letters with me on the subject of gun quality. Gunsmiths Jim and Roy Bedeaux of Albuquerque, who fix and modify my guns, have been sterling examples of common sense and craftsmanship. George Bird Evans treated my little AyA with the same respect I showed his priceless Purdey. Tom Davis, Steve Grooms, and Dave Petzal gave the first edition of this book critical reads.

A few gun dealers through the years indulged my fancies, gave me good deals, and allowed me to handle and even borrow guns I could not afford. The first among them, the man that gave me my earliest education in fine guns, is Charlie Callanan of Cambridge, Massachusetts. Since then, Ron Peterson of Albuquerque has gone beyond the limits of common sense to enable me to afford the guns I crave. Glenn Baker of Woodcock Hill, Anderson Bakewell, S.J., Larry Barnes of Gunnerman, Russell Chatham, Daniel Cote of the *Double Gun Journal*, Chuck Johnson of Wilderness Adventures, Datus Proper, and Richard Spilker have all provided help, information, and guns.

And special thanks to Steve Smith: all of the above, plus assignments, sympathy, and editing. Thanks, and good hunting!

Steve Bodio
Magdalena, NM

1

The Lure of Guns

I am a fine-gun addict, a user and a fan, but not a collector. I like sporting guns because they are tools that help us fit into the natural puzzle, and fine sporting guns because they are wonderful objects. If you are one who complains that guns kill things, you obviously shouldn't be reading this. They do, they should do it very well, and that's all I have to say about that. This book is for those who see a little magic in guns.

The matter of using versus collecting is important and needs some explanation. Guns these days are often considered a kind of art* rather than fine tools. I've been guilty.

When I lived in the East, I hunted grouse every fall, also woodcock. I always put in a little time on pheasant with my springer. I did some jump shooting, rather long range, for ducks in

---

*I prefer the word "craft" here to art, but that word has been debased until it is synonymous with "junk." I like a definition from John Barsness: "Art relates to the human condition; craft is everything else."

a steel shot-only marsh, some saltwater pass shooting on a then less-restricted sandbar, and, late in the season, some cold- weather wildfowling over decoys. I hunted deer with a shotgun, as required in Massachusetts, and promised myself I'd get to Maine and Vermont where I could use a rifle. Once I hunted turkey. What weapons would you say could justifiably be used by this hunter? Even given my gun-nut proclivities, I'd guess that one general 12, probably a good-quality double, given my tastes — plus one heavy 3-inch 12 pump for the marshes, or maybe a magnum 10, would cover it all. You *might* justify a light 20 or 28 for the early woodcock, a slug barrel for the pump for deer, and maybe even a rifle for Vermont, right?

Well, during the last ten years I spent in Massachusetts I owned an elegant 28-gauge Spanish double, three consecutive 20 gauge over-unders, two fancy French Darne side-by-sides, a Charlin built on the same patents in 16-gauge, a 20-gauge L.C. Smith, a 16-gauge Parker, a 12 ditto, a 16-gauge automatic Browning "Sweet Sixteen" for deer, two Sauer doubles in a case (only one worked, but the case was nice), a couple more beat up L.C. Smith 12s, a badly flawed model 21 Winchester, an Ithaca Mag 10 autoloader, an Ithaca 10 double from about 1915 with obsolete short chambers, and a collector-perfect Ithaca magnum 10 double from the thirties that had probably never been fired. I owned at least half of these at any one given time, despite an income driven down to literal poverty levels by my maniacal acquisitiveness. (I also owned a .22 magnum, a .250/3000, two .30/06s, a 7x57, and a .357 H&H magnum pre-'64 Model 70 that had seen service in Africa just in case I encountered Cape buffalo on Cape Cod.)

Was I happy with this awesome battery? Of course not! I was always worried about which one to use, why I couldn't hit with such and such, whether I should trade off the damned useless Sauer (but what should I put in the case?). If I went out and missed, I always blamed my choice of gun. I was trying to calculate what I could stand to lose against what I couldn't bear to live without. I was miserable. My life resembled a Gene Hill column. I was well on my way to becoming a collector and ignoring what guns were: tools, often elegant and craftsmanlike tools to be sure, but tools for all that.

Around that time, I fell into correspondence with George Bird Evans, the grand old grouse hunter, writer, and dog breeder of West Virginia. George is the ultimate "user." He does have two guns but the second, his famous Purdey, was left to him by Dr. Charles Norris. When he got it he wrote in awe: "I had shot my Fox for thirty-four years, and while no love affair lasts that long without a crisis, after the restocking job we were closer than ever and I had intended to continue shooting it as long as the two of us lasted. Now I possessed one of the finest guns made." George probably would have converted me to the path of virtue eventually, but real life did the job even faster. I decided to quit my job and go for broke, to devote all my time to freelance writing. Some of those guns had to go. Fast.

A few went well. I sold the Parker 16 to a friend, a magazine publisher who shot it and used it on the covers of brochures and a cookbook. I gave the Browning back to my father, who has probably killed more ducks with it than I ever will. But then, since I wanted whatever I had left to be perfect, I began to indulge in a new vice: trading. Trading is almost always a losing game for the non-professional. But it is educational if you like learning just what is wrong with your gun.

Some weird things happened. I sent the other Parker, which had slightly dented barrels, to a gunsmith who promptly refinished the barrels after wire-brushing them to a matte finish. He quartered the gun's worth in one operation and charged me for it. I left the French sliding-breech Charlin with another gunsmith, a friend, who promptly sold it for half what I paid for it. I found that some idiot had reamed out the chambers on that damned Model 21 to a dangerous 3½ inches and put a coat of bluing over an action rotted from the inside by saltwater rust.

And finally, I encountered and was tempted by the most insidious of all collector's dogmas: the cult of the unused. In my other field of accumulation, books, I have managed to stay honest. To me books are for reading. I like an old first edition as well as anybody, and since my parents were artists who raised me with an appreciation of such things, I love fine illustrations. But I am a writer first and foremost, and a cheap paperback is every bit as good as the leather-bound collector's item for the all-important *words.* I know that "reading copy" means something the dog ate half of. And I've always thought that it was a dumb attitude, like freeze-drying a banquet and putting it in storage to gloat over, while sneering at those who enjoy the "eater's version." But despite all this, I was still not immune to the cult of the new, unfired gun, to the contempt in a gun investor's voice as he dismissed a beloved heirloom Parker as a "good shooter" because of its silky gray, hand-rubbed finish.

Where I erred here was in selling, albeit for once at a profit, that old magnum 10 Ithaca. It had apparently been bought then put away in the late thirties by a sportsman who wanted one of everything. After he died it wandered from an estate sale, to a friendly dealer, to me. It looked as though it had just come out of the box, with 100% case colors, no bluing wear, and its plain finish intact. It was also the only graceful 10-gauge I have ever seen that was also heavy enough not to bash my face in every time I touched it off.

I should have kept it and shot it at turkeys and taken it to the sandbars where I would crouch with February sleet in my face watching for passing scoters. My forward hand would have eventually rubbed gray spots on the barrels; the case colors would have faded, and scratches would have appeared on the stock. But the old cannon was made for such treatment, and it never would have worn out in my lifetime, or for that matter, in my grandson's. I should have kept it and used it.

Instead, I fell prey to the keepers of the unused-gun flame. I wish I had read Delaware writer Bill Wise then: "...a bias in favor of mint, unaltered shotguns has been furthered by a few who buy and sell guns for a living or by the ultra-wealthy who stack high-priced guns away in vaults like so much cordwood." Every time I considered putting a recoil pad on the Ithaca, or shooting it anywhere near saltwater, somebody who knew better than I did would howl at me that it was a treasure, that doing this would be akin to painting a walrus mustache on the Mona Lisa. Finally, I sold it. It's one of the very few guns I regret selling; I feel that in taking it away from the salt marshes, I have committed a crime akin to locking up an eager hunting dog in a penthouse. Besides which, I'll never see its like at a decent price again.

Trading did teach me a few things, though, about differences in models, about defects in a seller's gun that you could use as bargaining points if you could conceal the "I want" in your own eyes, and about pure human sleazery — the kind that when you point out the unfixed crack in the stock says, "When did that happen?" or that tells you, of course you can shoot 3½-inch magnum shells in this here English 2½-inch chambered 10- gauge. Whether you *need* such cynicism and nit-picking anal retentiveness is another whole story.

But finally, there is a pure pleasure in acquisition of knowledge. Texas stockmaker and writer Dave Simpson once wrote to me, as I searched for the perfect game gun: "...discovery, not acquisition, is what collecting, and life, should be about." With this attitude I was finally able to get a Belgian sidelock 12 that was handmade in a small shop just before the First World War, with an English-type stock of Purdey-class wood, with gold plated interior works and sculpted fences, all for less than your average inflated Parker. Without the knowledge gained in accumulating and trading, I never would have had the nerve to buy it.

So what exactly are good guns? At a minimum, a good gun must be useful, beautiful, and well-made enough to last a lifetime. I would add a fourth quality that partakes of both useful and beautiful, but adds a little to them: "eumatic," an apt neologism best defined by its coiner, English gun authority Gough Thomas, as "the quality in a manually operated device whereby it is *totally* correlated to the human being who has to use it." Sometimes there's a fifth: the romance of history and association.

You don't have to have a million-dollar English "Best" to have a good gun. Thomas himself makes a case for the pump gun as a eumatic action — so much for British snobbery — although a lot of pumps don't measure up on the aesthetic and durability standards. The almost unknown sliding-breech French Darne gun beats the conventional break-action on a lot of grounds and is less expensive to make. Contrary to what some dealers will tell you, there are still good, affordable guns. On the other hand, all good guns are *relatively* expensive — handwork always is. You don't have to spend a year's salary, but you should get the best you can afford.

Romance? Of course! At its best, every good gun is a kind of time machine. Unlike other complex tools — unlike, say, even the best automobiles — guns don't break down with age. You can easily shoot your (or someone else's) grandfather's gun, and it will do as well for you as for him. An old gun will carry the toolmarks of long-dead craftsmen, the scars of hard hunts completed before you were born, the smooth patina left by the hands of an earlier generation. When today's hunters use such guns, they carry an extra magic that I cannot define, but must acknowledge. And if you acquire a good new gun, you are starting a chain that may extend into the future as long as hunters welcome the fall.

2

Two-Barreled Guns:
Principles and Prejudices

So, in this book of one man's prejudices, I intend to cover mostly sporting arms. There isn't a lot on black powder, because this is not a book about antiques or reproductions. Black powder guns are inevitably one or the other. There isn't anything on target guns because I use clay target games as a practice for hunting. You will see that I am biased in favor of doubles, of handwork, of genuine bargains. I don't like most repeating shotguns and have a mild bias in favor of single-shot rifles, though I have owned — and recommend — both the Model 12 and several bolt-action rifles. I hope you will enjoy my opinions, and that they will stimulate you to form your own.

And please: Don't think that an interest in quality is effete, a mere matter of status, or beside the point of hunting. A conscious hunter should know about his tools, and an aesthetic hunter should not be satisfied with junk. Hear, again, Gough Thomas: "There is an aesthetic quality in smooth, sweet action, responsive easy control, that recalls a bridle-wise horse with easy paces, as opposed to a hardmouthed brute that always seems to be travelling downhill."

Won't such qualities make you a better hunter?

Good guns are fine things, so perfect in their fusion of form and function that non, even anti-hunters, can be moved by their shape and grace. To want to own and use a few is a natural outcome of good hunting, related neither to conspicuous consumption nor to the neurotic "completionism" of collectors. Such a desire implies an intelligent and almost sensuous delight in the tools and craft of the sporting life.

Although my first hunting weapon was my father's 16-gauge Browning autoloading shotgun, the land-mine flushes favored by Massachusetts grouse and woodcock soon convinced me that the racy lines of the traditional side-by-side double, evolved almost biologically from two centuries of wingshooting, were more than merely aesthetic. Pumps and autoloaders descend mechanically from rifles, weapons meant to be *aimed*. But a good shotgun's function should be dynamic; it should sweep flying birds from the sky, pointing as naturally to its target as your finger does.

The lines of the basic double gun include two barrels set in a horizontal plane, a straight clean "wrist" known as the "English" grip, a minimal forend, and a high, straight stock. These lines appeared rather suddenly in early nineteenth-century England in the guns of the Manton brothers. Though many American writers will tell you that old guns have too much drop — that is, that they are too low at the butt-end for the shooter's convenience — they are thinking about heavy American models like early Parker and L.C. Smith duck guns. English upland guns from any time after 1820 have stocks you could shoot without alterations today. The main change in doubles has been from muzzle to breechloading, a change accomplished by 1880. Soon afterwards, most makers moved the hammers inside; since then, all changes have been mere refinements. Steel barrels became more reliable and replaced the formerly stronger and still prettier spirals of Damascus twist. London's testy maverick, Robert Churchill, shortened barrels from 30 inches to 25; other makers compromised at 26, 27, and 28 inches, today's standards.* But the basic design of the English stock has remained unchanged for 160 years, the action for a century.

Out here in the big game country of the West, you will hear riflemen complain that shotguns are not accurate. Of course they're not, at least if your standard for accuracy is a machine that punches dime-size holes in paper targets at a hundred yards! Damning shotguns because they don't ("Ah don't work on no shotguns; Ah only lahk accurate weapons.") is like calling an English setter worthless because it doesn't tree mountain lions. *It's not supposed to.*

But because of such prejudices, some American shotguns seem to approximate rifles in styling. First, we use repeaters. Second, we routinely shoot heavier loads than the English — more a matter of custom than from any ballistic reason — and therefore favor rifle-style pistol grips and paddle-like beavertail forends on the grounds that they "give the shooter something to hang onto." I can make a case for the beavertail, especially in gauges 20 and under. In such small guns, your fingers can obscure your sight when you wrap them around the slender barrels. But to me, the pistol grip is a mistake on most doubles; not only an aesthetic mistake, one that interferes with the ideal lines, but also a functional one. A pistol grip interferes with natural pointing and encourages rifle-style aiming.

You shouldn't necessarily shun repeaters because they are ugly or plebeian. you might well avoid them because they are ungainly, especially in the uplands, being too long and front-heavy; or because they are really more delicate than doubles in their mechanical complexity.

Some arguments in favor of doubles are ridiculous. A man once asked Jack O'Connor whether a double was a "gentleman's gun." O'Connor said yes, but went on to add that the possession of a gun with two barrels was scarcely the only requirement, something today's proliferating gun snobs might do well to remember. And the most commonly made argument in favor of doubles, the

---

*Although 26-inch barrels are often regarded as "standard" in the (usually heavier) American guns, *light* 27- or 28-inch barrels (more common in English and Continental guns) give a smoother swing and more natural balance.

"instant choice of chokes,"* has never seemed all that compelling to me. "Barrel-stretching" beyond fifty yards is a dubious proposition even with a tightly choked magnum; a cylinder bore barrel will mangle its target inside ten yards if you load it up with too much shot.

If American guns were choked like some European ones, in what amounts to wide open and very tight, you would have a real choice. But most American guns have two very similar chokes, and it doesn't make that much difference. For all but the closest and longest shots, you can scarcely go wrong with improved cylinder. The advantage of the double is simply that it gives you two shots, usually all you'll ever need ("one shot meat, two shots maybe, three shots heap shit," as the old saw goes) and gives them to you in a package that will enable you to shoot well.

Single triggers? They are easier to use with gloves, but double triggers are more versatile. On those rare occasions when you want to select another choke, it's a lot faster to pick the one you want by pulling the appropriate trigger than by fiddling with some kind of selector button. Besides, some popular single trigger mechanisms use the recoil of the first shot to set up the second; if your first shot misfires, you don't *get* a second. All in all, I'd say stick)with two triggers. Anybody who says he can't shift automatically from one trigger to the other hasn't tried. I am the world's least-coordinated human being, but I can get off my second shot, even on an early season ruffed grouse, with no conscious effort at all. An hour of dry practice should enable you to do the same.

Over-unders? I have owned two that I never should have sold, a 20-gauge Ruger and a Merkel 12. But unless you can afford thirty-thousand-dollar Bosses and Lebeau-Courallys, over-unders are rarely as graceful as side-by-sides. Even at that rarefied level, they usually are heavier than their side-by-side counterparts, though except in guns that will be used in heavy cover, this may not be as great a fault as we have been brainwashed into thinking. An

---

*Need I define choke? OK. Choke is a minute constriction at the muzzle end of the barrel, designed to tighten the pattern and enable you to hit farther away, on the same principle that makes a stream of water from a hose narrow down when you compress it. Chokes range from cylinder (none) through improved cylinder (not much) and modified (some) to full (a lot) of constriction.

even smaller point against them is that it is damn near impossible to get one with two triggers, at least in the United States.

(The final complaint quoted against over-unders, the greater gape required to open one, is not an issue. The only place it makes any difference is in a duck blind, and if you're grabbing shells, you might as well stand up — the ducks will see you anyway.)

There might be something said in favor of the over-under's single sighting plane, though it goes against my "don't aim, just point and swing" semiconscious, natural theory of hitting. If everything else that you have ever shot had a single sighting plane — that is, if you previously shot rifles and repeaters — it will look familiar and that may make a difference. Also, clay shooters like over-unders because they give a better view of rising targets. It is best to get familiar with one sort of sighting image. Of course all these rules are made to be broken. Use what works. (Ignore side-by-side snobs like me who will occasionally refer to over-unders as "yuppie sticks.")

About here, I should define the words "sidelock" and "boxlock."

Sidelock guns have the longer pedigree and are rather harder to make, and so are often automatically considered more "aristocratic." In them, the locks or operating mechanisms of the action (as in "lock, stock, and barrel") are detachable units, attached to the insides of plates, which in turn are fitted to the sides of the gun. "Jaws" of wood extend forward above and below each plate. Think of the appearance of hammer guns. Sidelocks are not truly "hammerless"; indeed, no double is. The makers have simply moved the hammers inside the lockplates. In "bar action" sidelocks — most common today — the locks are powered by flat springs set in a tongue that extends forward into the action bar. "Back action" sidelocks lack this extension and are therefore considered the stronger, since there is no need to remove metal in the bar. They are most common in old English elephant rifles and big-bore duck guns, often in combination with external hammers.

The boxlock is a rugged mechanism invented by Anson and Deeley, two gunsmiths employed by Westley Richard, in 1875. (It is therefore often called the "Anson & Deeley" action.) Here the locks

Sidelock

and hammers are completely enclosed in a squarish body. Usually it is joined to the stock wood by a more or less vertical line, though this may be embellished by curves or scallops. The boxlock action is cheaper to make than the sidelock because there is less need to inlet the wood. It is often lighter because there is less metal. Except for these obvious differences, there is no inherent difference in quality between boxlock and sidelock guns, despite what snobs may tell you. Sidelocks are a little prettier in line and stronger, and have more space for engraving,* but for the same money, you'll usually get a better boxlock than a sidelock.

I should add that hard-core sidelock fans, including some good friends, insist that trigger pulls are better on sidelocks. If this is true, the difference is hard to detect, at least to my crude perceptions.

Regardless of type, doubles are surrounded by high-cost image and mindless snobbery. Don't be afraid. The classic double

---

*Because of this difference, some makers outfit their boxlocks with plates that resemble sidelocks for decoration. *These are not sidelock guns!* One of my pet peeves is the designation "full sidelock" used to differentiate the true sidelock from these side-plate guns. There are no "half" sidelocks, only sidelocks and boxlocks and a few oddities like sliding-breech guns and round-actions.

Boxlock

gun is simply the most efficient weapon that you can use to kill birds. The straight stock is designed for pointing; it is carved from aged walnut, chosen not just for its gorgeous patterns and contrasting colors, but because it is strong enough to withstand recoil and dense enough to receive the checkering. The checkering itself is there to aid your grip. The dead-black bluing is armor against rust, and the rainbow colors on the action are a byproduct of the necessary hardening process. Even the engraved scrolls have a purpose: They break up the flat reflective surfaces of the gun.

Despite some dealers' efforts to promote a cult of rarity and high price around certain names, there is a double available to suit every budget. Embellishment is gravy; look for the meat: dense wood, sharp checkering, fine lines, balance, and tightness. Don't let anybody talk you into anything. Use your eyes, your brain, and your own good common sense.

3

America's Classic Shotguns

Before we pass on to individual makers, we should look at a few shotgun fundamentals. First, "gauge." Gauge is an archaic measurement: the number of lead balls of the same diameter as the bore or inside diameter of the gun barrel that it takes to equal one pound. To take the most obvious example, the 16-gauge has a bore diameter identical to that of a one-ounce sphere of lead. The smaller the gauge number, the larger the bore. Today, we shoot gauges of 28, 20, 16, 12, and 10 — or as the English say, "bores." We also have .410 *caliber* shotguns, that is, guns in which the bore measures .41 inch.

I'm not partisan on gauges. I don't like .410s, partly because they are notorious cripplers unless you are abnormally disciplined and knowledgeable about range (you must shoot well within 35 yards to be safe), partly because I can barely hit the ground with them. I like 28s (which, despite their small size, are more akin ballistically to the 20 than the .410), and 12s, and have a long on-and-off affair with the 10. I like the 16 and lament its neglect; most American shooters think it is old-fashioned and redundant, falling as it does between the 20 and the 12. It's really more of a golden mean, especially for upland hunting. Besides, 16s are currently bargains because of their neglect, although that is changing.

The so-called "magnum" chambered guns are common in America. In order to stuff in more powder and shot, magnum 12s, 20s, and .410s are all made with chambers three inches long rather than the standard 2¾ inches (2½ in standard .410). Such long-chambered guns are probably less efficient and balanced than ones equipped with the standard chambers. You might make an argument for the 10-gauge in its magnum 3½-inch version. America does not allow you to hunt migratory birds with the 8-gauge, considered the standard for goose shooting in England, and the magnum 10 shoots an 8-bore's 2 or 2½ ounces of shot. That's what magnums are — attempts to load amounts of shot more suitable for larger gauges into smaller ones. The 28 and the 16 have kept to traditional balanced loads and standard chambers, which is another reason to like them.

Let me elaborate a bit here. If I were faced with the choice of one shotgun for all my hunting, it would be either a 16 or an "English" 12. This does not mean a gun from England; it means a 12 that weighs no more than 6½ pounds and "balances" with standard English-type shot charges of 1⅛ ounces or less of shot. Such loads will kill anything efficiently in the uplands and have always served well for decoying ducks — will again, when non-toxic loads made from substances other than steel shot become widely available. In fact, they'll do for all shotgunning other than for passing wildfowl and turkey that hang out beyond forty yards. The one-ounce 16-gauge load has virtually the same effect in the real world; a gun for it should weigh no more than 6 pounds.

Americans have traditionally crammed more shot into their guns (and therefore carried heavier guns, for less distracting recoil) than Europeans. The independent American hunter could often afford only one gun, and he shot a lot of big birds with it. Nowadays, when loads are more efficient for their weight and shots are fewer, we are beginning to appreciate European-type guns and loads. There are plenty of guns built in the golden age of American shooting that conform to this description; just pay attention to the weights given above. You are a little more likely to find one in a 16.

Also, give some thought to English 2½-inch shells for 12- and 16-gauges; they are becoming more available in the U.S. Shells shorter than chambers (see below) cause no harm, and the efficient low-recoil loads may make you a fan. Use them with open chokes. (Open the chokes.) An American load that is nearly equivalent for the 12 is the Winchester 1¹/₈ ounce "Superlight." It is also a good load for real English guns.

Chamber length is one of the most maddening aspects of old-gun study. These days, matters are simple, at least in the United States: .410s are still available in a 2½-inch length, and 10s and 12s in 3½ inches; all the other gauges use either the 2¾-inch chamber or, in magnum, the 3 inch. (This *is* simple!) Unfortunately some buyers assume that this has always been so.

But consider: As I have said, English guns may have chambers of 2 inches (.410) and 2½ inches (28, 20, 16, *and* 12). American guns used the 2½-inch length in the 28 and 20; the American 16 had a chamber of 2⁹/₁₆ inches; the 12, 2⁵/₈. While most shooters know enough not to use 3½-inch magnum 10-gauge ammunition in a 2³/₄ standard-chambered gun, they may not realize that in many, perhaps most, 10-gauges made before the mid-1920s, the chambers are only 2⁵/₈ inches.

What difference do these fractions make? Often, plenty. When the crimp at the front end of a shotshell doesn't have room to unfold, pressure can build to a damaging degree. While this should not cause a barrel-burst in a gun with unaltered chambers, it can shorten the life of your gun, loosen the action, even crack the gun at the angle of the water table and the standing breech.* Some dealers will glibly assure you that chambers can be lengthened, but doing so can weaken the barrels or allow use of cartridges more powerful than the gun was built to handle, resulting in the same problems that you would encounter using too-long shells.

What to do? First, know your chamber length — get gauges, and check the chamber length stamped on the barrel flats (2¾ inches = 70mm) on Continental guns. Second, if you want to

---

*That is, at the angle between the horizontal and vertical planes of the action.

shoot a short-chambered gun, buy or build appropriate ammunition. 2½-inch English cartridges are now available in gauges 28 through 12, and you can even order the 2-inch 12, for special English featherweights, from some dealers.

The final alternative, to lengthen chambers, is a last resort (which may ruin you gun). I would not lengthen chambers on an English gun, especially one of fine quality; British "proof" testing already enables the makers to shave what metal they can, and to remove more is unsafe. In England, you cannot legally sell a gun with lengthened chambers unless you pay to send it for re-proofing first. On American guns, at least use common sense. Going from $2^5/8$ to 2¾ ($2^6/8$) isn't *too* radical a step; going from 2½ to 3 inches would be both ridiculous and dangerous. Is this subject worth this much bother? Let me put it this way: Neither your forward hand, nor a cracked action, can be repaired.

Early American doubles — defined simply as those double guns built in the United States before the Second World War — have achieved a sort of cult status related less to their beauty and function than to snobbery and the nostalgia they evoke. The status supposedly conferred by owning such a double is akin to the "gentleman's gun" phenomenon noted by O'Connor; the nostalgia exists because we imagine the time when these guns were made to be simpler, a sort of golden age of shotgunning. Both are poor reasons to own one. Virtually all the American doubles are good guns, especially if you can get one in good working condition for a reasonable price, but none is a sacred icon, a Rolls- Royce, not (for the most part) even a Westley Richards. When a dealer asks $2,000 for a VH Parker, you'd be better off buying an AyA.

Still, there are some good reasons to own one of "ours."

The first, most desired, and most inflated of the old Yankee guns is the Parker. While a certain class of gun buyer gets positively horny at the sight of the Parker's distinctive eye-like hingepin, filling the air with cries of "Old Reliable!" and "America's finest shotgun!" the Parker really is nothing more than a simple, intelligently designed, extremely well-finished boxlock. But this "nothing more" encompasses a square-edged "doll's head" extension from the rib, one of the best ways to strengthen the boxlock design. The "bite" in the lugs under the barrel is topped with a plate that can be replaced to tighten the gun when it becomes worn. The whole gun is well-balanced — the action, which rests between your hands, is short and massive, giving the Parker that magical dynamic action so desired by knowledgeable shotgunners.

But to my mind, where the Parker really excels is in its incredible choice of options, especially gauges and action sizes. All American shotguns were built in varying grades of ornamentation and wood quality. All were made in at least 20-, 16-, and 12-gauges; all had choices of single triggers or double, splinter forend or beavertail, pistol grip or straight, and so on. But Parker built guns in every gauge from .410 to 8 — hammerless 8 at that! They made guns in magnum 10, though most people think only Ithaca did. They introduced the 28-gauge to America, and popularized it. (Parker-o-philes who think they *invented* it should read any edition of Greener's *The Gun and Its Development*.) The Parker Company didn't just fit different-gauge barrels to two or three different frames, but built guns on almost as many size frames as gauges: six, ranging from dainty triple-0's with milled-out depressions in the water table to remove weight, to number threes for magnum 10s and 8s. Nor were these frames necessarily confined to single gauges. I have owned a featherweight 16 built on the 0 frame, normally used for 20-gauge, and seen a 16-gauge heavy duck gun with 32-inch barrels on the number 2, or standard 12 frame. The first gun weighed less than six pounds; the second, eight pounds eight ounces!

Parker's finish also surpassed that of most other American classics. While its competitors lavished scroll and precious metals on their higher-grade guns, the effect was often garish or even grotesque — L.C. Smith's gold lightning bolts on the barrels come to mind. Fox was better, but except on the very highest-grade Ithacas, the engraving on American guns was comparatively crude. *All* the Parker grades look good. They went from no engraving on the Trojan — incidentally not the "true" Parker action, but a simplified cheaper version — through a simple border on the V grade, up through increasing amounts of English-quality scroll, to some truly lavish specimens in the B and A grades.

For my mind, the best bargains have always been in the D grades or thereabouts — enough decoration and fine wood to be attractive, but slightly below the level that attracts the most savage of Parker vultures. The scroll is consistently the best on any American gun; its only possible rival is that on high-level side-plate Lefevers, but these are much rarer (and, usually, heavier and more fragile) guns. The animal engraving — dogs and such — is not perfect on Parkers. But then, it isn't always better on a brand-new Holland & Holland.

All of which would seem to say that Parkers are worth what the dealers are asking. Unfortunately, there are some drawbacks. First, Parkers are notorious for being hard-kicking guns. This may have something to do with short forcing cones or chambers, but probably is mainly a result of stock design. Parkers tend toward low combs except in trap grades. Add to this a sort of sharp-edged profile and the lightweight frame (the second a virtue in a gun with a straighter stock), and you have a recipe for bruised cheekbones and a flinch. The triggers also seem closer together than on some doubles, and Parker never adopted the European practice of hinging the front trigger to fold forward (articulate) when it touches the shooter's finger during recoil from the second barrel. A trigger-finger bruise can hurt more than one on a cheekbone or shoulder. That light 16 was tolerable with light loads, but it was always a kicker, perhaps the second worst I ever owned.

But the worst thing about Parkers is the idiotic inflation. Apparently, every pretentious shooter knows that this one American "name" is a safe bet to impress his like-minded friends. (If he were richer he would automatically buy a Purdey, even if he could get a better deal on, say, a Dickson round action; his car is a BMW, his sour mash Jack Daniels, his running shoes Reeboks — you *know* he has running shoes....) And he thinks of his Parker — probably a light 12, hard-kicking, plain-finished VHE — as an "investment," even though he paid some "name" dealer $2200 for it. Don Zutz has his number. In *The Double Shotgun* he states: "If somebody buys a Parker for an outrageous price, will he be able to find an even greater fool to take it off his hands for even more money in the future? Sooner or later the traffic won't bear higher prices."

Parkers are neither fine art nor, unless you are lucky enough to find the fabled missing "Invincible" in your attic, an investment. At their best, they are good, honest Yankee guns, built to give both years of service and a little aesthetic satisfaction. My favorite Parker might be a VHE 12 owned by the father of a grouse-hunting friend, a businessman from a Boston family. Since it's a brush gun, he unceremoniously cut the barrels back to 24 inches. The rainbow colors on the receiver are gone, leaving the old-silver patina only achieved by decades of use. Reed tells of a time when his father shot with it at a fancy club, where "all the members had Purdeys." It was, he remembers, "the right gun for a grouse hunter from Boston."

You know, I'd rather have *that* Parker than one with ten gold inlays.

I should say something about the "new Parker," the one briefly made under Winchester backing in Japan, and, though no longer being manufactured, still available. This gun, officially known as The Parker Reproduction, just might be your best bet in Parkers, if you can afford the stiff $3,000-plus price. It is such a careful reproduction that the parts will interchange with original guns built in Meriden, Connecticut. But the metal is stronger, and, best of all, it's available in both 28- and 16-gauges. Twenty-eight-gauge Parkers are rare and special guns, carried by such shotgunning legends as grouse maven William Harnden Foster and ornithologist-writer William Beebe. Even in the utilitarian VH grade, they will likely cost you more than $3,000; since 28-gauges were never common, there is, for once, some justification for the high price.

The new Parkers are all of the scroll-engraved D grade or above. You can order yours with the elegant skeleton buttplate, a neatly inletted metal frame that surrounds an expanse of checkered wood. The stock dimensions are good, and the 28 is the lightest kicking of all the useful gauges. A single trigger is available. My only reservation, a personal taste, is the claro walnut — it's showy, but a bit coarse for fine checkering.

The second most famous of the old doubles is probably the L.C. Smith gun, America's only well-known sidelock, manufactured by the Hunter Arms Company. In the middle grades especially, it is an exceptionally handsome gun, with the sweeping lines that cause gun nuts to swoon over sidelocks. But at the risk of being lynched by the "Elsie's" legion of fans, I think it is an overrated piece.

The L.C. has two design faults that offset its many virtues: its stocks crack, and its back-action sidelocks lack the intercepting sears common to almost all English and Continental hammerless sidelocks, which keep the gun from going off as a result of an accidental jar. If you somehow manage to drop an L.C. on its butt, it may well go off. Of course, it's too easy to say you shouldn't *do* this....

The cracking is less dangerous but probably more annoying. Most L.C. Smith guns, especially 12-gauges, eventually develop hairline cracks behind the lockplates. These can grow until the gun is unsafe to shoot. Some say that as the quality of wood and workmanship increases, the likelihood of cracks decreases, but I have seen at least one cracked Crown grade, a very fancy gun indeed. Shotgun authority and author Michael McIntosh lays the blame on the rectangular, rather than bevelled, edges on the lockplates, and says that a good stockmaker can fix the problem by slightly undercutting the inletting behind them.

In the late sixties, the Marlin Company revived the L.C. Smith field-grade guns, but just a little too soon to catch the wave of double-gun popularity. Snooty collectors scorn the Marlin Smiths. Ironically, not only is the Marlin L.C. a "true" Smith — like the new Parker, its parts are interchangeable with the early "genuine" guns — but Marlin found another solution to the stock cracks: their designers inletted a strip of fiberglass under the locks where they contacted the wood. Therefore, the scorned Marlin Smiths are a bargain for anybody who wants to shoot America's sidelock, often available for as little as $400 — and of course, because they are newer, they tend to be in good condition. Before you run out to look for one, be aware that there aren't many Marlin Smiths around, and those that do exist are all stout, plain, tight-choked 12s, more suitable for duck and turkey than quail.

The L.C. has its particular virtues as well. Like all back-action sidelocks, it is extremely strong; 3-inch magnum Smiths make great duck, goose, and turkey guns. Its much-advertised rotary bolt system is as good a lockup as anyone has ever designed. I won't go so far as some partisans, who claim they have never seen a loose L.C., but the rotary bolt's automatic compensating action makes for fewer loose guns than most other old American shooters.

I do not want to sound anti-L.C., only realistic. My first good double was a 20-gauge, field-grade Smith, and it was a sweet little gun. An old friend, a commercial fisherman, shoots grouse with a late Hunter Arms field grade 12 that has never cracked. He got it from a Vermont farmer in the late sixties, in trade for seventy-five dollars and a roll of carpet. It is as tight as the day it was made.

The most exotic of the old American actions is the Lefever, in both its early side-plate form and in its extremely rare Anson & Deeley configuration. The side-plate Lefever is a handsome and also a very strange gun. At first glance it resembles a sidelock. But if you remove its lockplates, you will find that they are mere covers for a sort of exposed variant of the boxlock mechanism. Why more gunmakers have not followed this pattern I do not know, for it makes for both beauty and far more convenience in access to the working parts than most Anson & Deeley guns.

These guns have other oddities, most of which are also virtues, though I shudder to think of what the cost of making them would be today. Cocking is accomplished by a hook that sticks up from the action, allowing a very solid bar. All choking was custom. Many of the moving parts are fitted with takeup screws that can be turned to compensate for wear. When Lefever moved on to form another company, he kept the cocking hook and the "compensating" action in a new gun that more closely resembled a conventional A&D action. But all the Lefever guns are designers' dreams, and gunsmiths' nightmares. The workmanship on them often surpasses even Parker's.

Shotgun expert Don Zutz thinks the Lefevers, especially the side-plate types, are the best bargains of all old American guns. I'm not quite so certain, though my reservation has little to do with the quality of Lefever design. The trouble with Lefevers is that they are *old*. Production ceased on the "boxlock" Lefevers in 1906; the side-plate jobs hung on until 1915. While they were made to last, you should remember that more Lefevers were built with Damascus barrels than fluid steel, and that virtually all the steel-barreled guns have *short chambers*. (I recently read an article about two missing top-grade Lefever side-plate 10s in a national magazine that described them as having 2⅞-inch chambers. Maybe — but I've yet to see a Lefever 10 with chambers longer than 2⅝.) If you are the kind of person who is comfortable with such things, you could lengthen the chambers. But the steel made in 1915 was not necessarily as strong as that in other high-grade American doubles, all of which made it to World War II.*

Caveat emptor. I would have no reservations about buying an old Lefever. But I'd shoot it with short, original-strength loads. And if I were unwilling to do the work of "rolling my own," I'd regretfully leave it on the dealer's shelf.

By the way — none of these remarks apply to the so-called Lefever Nitro Special (made by Ithaca, who bought out the company) or the late thirties "Ithaca Lefever." The former was a rugged if very plain boxlock of conventional design, often available even today for less than $400. The second was an Ithaca with very different trim — sort of like a GMC and a Chevy pickup truck.

I thaca is America's plain-Jane boxlock, the working man's good double. There's little innovation here, other than the invention of the magnum 10-gauge (probably a conscious effort to get around the purely cosmetic federal ban on gauges of 8 and above for wildfowling). Ithacas have boxy silhouettes, coarse engraving (except on the legendary thousand-dollar grade), and were probably the least expensive of the good American guns. They were also rugged, simple, featured a fast lock time that made them a favorite of competition shooters like Annie Oakley, and were available in gauges from .410 through 28 to magnum 10. They were the gun of choice, I think, for their time's equivalent of the readers of this book, hardworking hunters who knew quality but were not rich.

---

*I have seen terrifying pictures of an exploded Lefever 10-gauge in which someone had lengthened the chambers.

Elmer Keith, a plain man and a gunner's gunner, carried the first magnum 10, made originally for Major Charles Askins, for nearly fifty years.

Listen to John McDaniels on his hunting partner's Ithaca (from *The Turkey Hunter's Book*): "The gun is not as pretty as a Purdey but this is an American gun. It was made for honest, decent men who were not born of notable lineage...It is a reminder of a period when fine American shotguns were made by hand, by men who cared."

That's the Ithaca. If you like history, you might enjoy knowing that Ithaca's catalogs of the thirties were illustrated by the great bird artist Louis Agassiz Fuertes. I've got one of them. Now does anyone out there have an Ithaca double $2^7/_8$-inch 10 for sale?

Potential Ithaca users, as opposed to collectors, should probably confine themselves to the "New Ithaca Double" or NID, the gun made after 1925. Ithaca extended chambers to modern lengths in 1924, but there were already signs that smokeless powder was too strong for the older designs and metals. Pre-NID guns have thin fences and a sliding cocking piece on the bottom of the barrel lump; they also have conventional "bites" in the lumps. NID have the doll's head and rotary bolt as their only locking device; they are chunkier, more substantial-looking guns. From their introduction until the mid-thirties, they also featured cocking indicators — stubby little rods that projected from the top of the action and retracted when the gun was fired. If you have any doubt about whether your prospective purchase is an NID, ask the dealer. If he can't answer, don't buy it.

I should also mention the Ithaca trap gun here. It was a massive-actioned single barrel that hung on into the 1970s. At least one English designer thinks that it and the next gun are the only American designs worth owning!

T he A.H. (Ansley) Fox guns of Philadelphia are the last of America's truly classic side-by-sides. They were simple, rugged boxlocks, with a graceful profile more like that or an English gun than the other American boxlocks. Fox had a rather more inflated idea of his gun than the designers at Ithaca did of theirs; many contemporary ads proclaim that the Fox is, "The finest gun in the world!"

Such bombast is — well — advertising. But it shouldn't blind the prospective buyer to the Fox's real virtues. For one thing, most Foxes I have seen are finished to a higher standard than any Ithaca. The wood, especially on the high grades, is gorgeous European walnut — a feature shared only by the high-grade Parkers and Lefevers among American makers. European walnut is denser, harder, and shows better contrast than American. And for some reason, Foxes tend to show up in better shape than working-grade Parkers, L.C.s, and Ithacas, perhaps an unintentional but pleasing outcome of a little — shall we say — snobbery in their first owners.

A good Fox gun to watch for is the H-E grade magnum, a 3-inch 12-gauge wildfowl gun with over-bored barrels. Boring barrels to a larger inside diameter than normal lightens pressures, improves patterns, and increases the effect of choke. Nash Buckingham's famous Burt Becker magnum "Bo Whoop" was a handmade example of the Fox 3-inch gun.

Other advantages? Foxes have fewer moving parts than other American doubles and so have fewer things to go wrong. Like the Ithaca NID, they use coil springs, which unlike leaf springs often continue to function even after they are broken.

Disadvantages? Very few! The Fox's hammers do not rebound, and so firing pins can occasionally get stuck in a primer, making the gun hard to open.

If you can find a Fox — they are rarer than Parkers, Ithacas, and L.C. Smiths — it will likely give you years of satisfaction, as well as romantic associations.* After all, its fans have included Theodore Roosevelt, Nash Buckingham, and George Bird Evans.

I will not dwell on one other classic American action, the Remington Model 32 over-under of the 1930s. I am not ignoring the vertical double, but in practice this bulky gun was used far more for target shooting than for hunting. The same was true of its short-lived descendant, the 3200, introduced in 1973 and dropped a few years later; it was a heavy gun, not suitable for carrying all day in cover. One possible exception would be the 3200 waterfowl magnum. This gun was just as heavy as the other models, if not

---

*As this book goes to press, a new version of the Fox, in 20-gauge only, has been revived in Connecticut. Prices start at $5000.

more so, but was the first double built specifically for use with steel shot. They're all ugly.

T he last of the famous American doubles to make its entrance was born in 1941 and still hangs on today in an opulent, over-priced version, like some almost-extinct species. Winchester's fabled Model 21 is a maddening gun, a product of some genius that sells for more than many cars, a classic example of the engineering principle of "overdesign," a slab-sided, clunky creation that in the words of one friend possesses a certain honest "blunt glamour," or at least did before it was dressed in baroque gold dogs and *fleur-de-lis* carvings.

The 21 was a very plain-looking gun when it was first pre-sented, free of any decoration or engraving, with unfigured wood and double triggers. Its marvels were all on the inside — incredibly strong chrome-moly steel, chopper lump barrels — that is, ones with each lug machined integrally with its barrel — linked by a ver-tical dovetail, an adjustable "bite," a lockup that resisted an aston-ishing torture test consisting of shooting 2,000 overpowered proof loads! The 21 might be the most rugged action ever made in America.

In fact, it may well be *too* rugged. No 21 has ever been accused of being a graceful or featherweight gun, and its square-edged flat surfaces have often served as targets of scorn for English gun writers. Nobody at Winchester ever seems to have asked why anyone would want to shoot the kind of loads that the 21 was designed to resist.

Still, some mid-period 21s are probably as close to the mythical all-around gun, especially for a versatile American shooter, as anything else. You can fire light loads in the uplands, then take the same gun out with heavy cartridges for casual duck or long-range pheasant, neither damaging the gun nor (because of its inevitable weight) kicking yourself silly. So called "skeet" grades — probably used more in upland hunting than on any skeet field — are especially handsome and useful: moderately light, short-bar-reled,* often with English grips, checkered butts, and handsome

*This is a virtue _only_ in a heavy gun!

American walnut. The 16 is exceptionally well-balanced, and 3-inch 20s on the same frames, heavy enough to absorb the surprisingly sharp kick of the little magnum shell, also deserve their popularity.

Another good 21, if you can find it, is the 3-inch heavy duck gun, a massive 12 with a well-designed beavertail and single trigger that might just be the best and most reliable American duck gun ever built. Remember, it was made to be a workhorse. Don't hang it on the wall.

The 21s "easy open" feature (the gun uses a spring in the lump to pop the barrels down as soon as you push the opening lever to the side) is still another nice touch, common in European guns but often scorned by ignorant gun buyers ("This gun's *loose*"). I have never seen a loose 21.

If you can find a double trigger 21 — they are all old, plain guns — you will probably have a bargain on your hands because of this feature alone. Incredibly, nobody wants them. Avoid .410s and 28s (if you can afford their $10,000 prices!). They have skinny little barrels sticking out of the chunky square 20-gauge action, likes pencils stuck in a matchbox, and have about as much balance. As for the gold-inlaid '59 Cadillac-style Grand Americans, I'll let my occasionally surreal correspondent Randy Davis speak: "They look real good with jukeboxes."

There is one more indisputable contender for the title "American Classic," and it's not a double. Let me admit it right up front: I hate repeaters. Most of them are clanking, unbalanced hunks of stamped metal. They look like the misbegotten bastards of military and sporting arms they are; if they are autoloaders, they jam; if they are pump actions, they won't jam but if you stress them too hard, they will *break*. (Don't yell at me about the ruggedness of pumps; I hunt with some hard-core wildfowlers; one has broken two pumps in the last three years, and they weren't bargain-basement brands either. They were both repairable, but not in the field.) What's more, they don't open in a simple manner so you can see down the barrels and make sure they are not loaded or clogged. They're not safe.

And yet — there is one repeater, a pump at that, I can love: Winchester's wonderful Model 12, a gun first brought out in 20-gauge in 1912, that lasted until the seventies, that is machined from the same fine steels as the 21 that lasts forever; a gun so graceful that *Englishmen* love it. Hear the ultra-respectable Geoffrey Boothroyd, gun columnist for the English *Shooting Times and Country* magazine, a man whose taste is so refined, he shoots a Dickson round action: "The Winchester Model 12, for example, cannot be faulted in its styling whereas the much vaunted Winchester Model 21 double is, in my eyes, *truly ugly*, [italics mine] regardless of how much gold inlay, engraving, and fancy wood is used for the stock."

Kidding aside, the 12 is one of the world's great guns. It is conceivably the only graceful repeater ever made, with sweeping curves and machined connections that are, sadly, too expensive to make any more at a truly reasonable price. The pump action is a natural one for a shooter to use; as the gun recoils, it is "eumatic" to move the slide forward then back, to fill the chamber. I have used two different Model 12s, my father's 16-gauge when I was a kid, and a plain-grade 12-gauge. Neither has ever malfunctioned, not once. (My father's Sweet Sixteen Belgian Browning automatic, a John M. Browning-designed action that is the only other repeater that could conceivably qualify as a classic, used to jam at least once every other season.)

Another advantage of the M12 for the poor shooter with taste is that so many were made that there is one for every budget. (Twenty-eight gauges are not for the poor, however; the last one I saw for sale was very plain, and they wanted over $2000.) The Model 12 was never made in .410, but the almost identical Model 42 was, for those of you who have to hunt with popguns.

Browning has recently taken advantage of new technology by reviving many old Winchester designs, both Model 12s and rifles, at affordable prices. The Model 12 is now available in 20 and 28-gauges, and a Model 42-type in .410. All these have modern steel and, to my mind, are as good as the originals, if without their collector value. If I had the dollars, I'd be seriously tempted by a 28-bore for doves.

Disadvantages? I wish it were easier to look through the barrel. One's inability to do so is the biggest inherent disadvantage of repeaters. And yet — damn! — I used to hit better with my M12 than with any of my doubles. And I shoot mostly doubles.

Are there any other "American Classic" shotguns being made today? Maybe. I would give a tentative nod to William Ruger's over-under. I think, despite the fact that it's rather heavy, that it is the only great vertical double ever built in America, and it may be getting better.

The Ruger is an unconventional over-under, with its locking lugs beside the barrels like those on good British and Italian guns. The absence of projections beneath the barrels gives the Ruger a trim, shallow profile unlike, say, the fat Belgian Browning with it's underlug system. Like the Winchester Model 21, the gun is an "easy opener," popping instantly to its full gape as soon as you thumb the lever to the right. Like the M21 it is criticized by the ignorant for being "loose."

Because Bill Ruger (our ranking genius of sporting firearm design, a man with a better eye than John Browning ever possessed) prefers simplicity to garish dress, the Ruger is above all a *clean* gun. It features lush curves, a stark smooth surface free of pins and screws and also the hard rectangles of the similarly plain 21, good wood, simple checkering, and a solid red recoil pad. Its sole fault is that, because of the American propensity for shooting overpowering loads, it is too heavy, especially in 20-gauge.

But what the hell; at around a thousand dollars, it's still one of the best buys in double guns that exists: handsome, rugged, and a precise pointer. In fifty years, people will be gobbling up Rugers the way they do the good old guns now. Or maybe not—for probably Ruger will still be making them. There is a stainless-steel 12-gauge — what a splendid idea for a waterfowl gun! — and a beautifully balanced, over-bored sporting clays gun. A trim and slightly lighter straight-grip model is available. Now if we could just persuade Mr. Ruger to design a 28-gauge side-by-side....

There are a few other contenders for the title "Classic American Shotgun." But they are or were all built elsewhere, in either Belgium or Japan, and so belong in another chapter. The guns above all deserve the title. Whatever my opinions, you can scarcely go wrong with any of them, especially if you use them for their intended purposes.

4

Big Bores

But it was the other shotgun that was really fabulous...It was a magnum 10 gauge double with barrels thirty-three inches long and weighed just under fourteen pounds. No man but the captain, it was said, could take the punishment it dealt the shoulder in a day in a duck blind, and on the still damp foggy air of a good duck day in the marshes it could be heard for miles, like the boom of a cannonade.

—William Humphrey, *Home From the Hill*

This wonderful passage for William Humphrey's 1957 novel embodies the mythological lure as well as the imagined deficiencies of the big-bore shotgun. To the average American hunter, the 10-gauges (and the 8s, 4s, and punt guns) are dinosaurs, romantic relics, slightly evil tools used on the great wildfowl flocks of a vanished golden age. On the one hand, you will hear that their kick is enough to disable the shooter, that their weight makes them impossible to carry and difficult to swing. On the other hand, ever since Nash Buckingham's famous 1960 essay "Are We Shooting Eight-Gauge Guns?" many gun writers have bought the idea that today's 3-inch magnum 12-gauges carry more shot than the old 8-bore load, or that the difference in range between the 12 and the 10 is so small that the 10's advantage is canceled by its increased weight and expense.

All of which is misleading, if not just plain wrong. Ten-gauges are uniquely useful guns, perhaps more so than ever since the advent of steel shot. They can carry more shot than any 12. They pattern better with 12-gauge loads than most 12s do, because their bigger bores deform fewer pellets and allow less shot "stringing." They handle the large shot sizes necessary to retain down-range energy with steel pellets. And in a properly constructed gun, their recoil is no worse, and may even be less sharp, than a magnum 12's.

To understand the virtues of the modern magnum 10, it helps to know something about the 8-gauge, a great wildfowling gun that has been an outlaw in the United States for two generations. Contrary to conventional wisdom, the 8 enjoys real popularity to this day in England; in fact, it is in the midst of a revival. Eights have always been made, except for a short gap in the 1950s and 1960s. As early as 1910, they carried anything from 2¼ ounces — the so-called light 8! — to three ounces of large shot, thereby *even then* exceeding the two-ounce upper limit of the heaviest, most modern magnum 12. Finally, the 8-gauge makes a more balanced firearm for the 2½-ounce-plus load than any 10-gauge.

I'm afraid most of Mr. Buck's statistics only hold true for muzzleloaders. Despite his claims, I doubt that any breechloading 8 was ever built to fire less than two ounces of shot. The turn-of-the-century English waterfowler was either a rich amateur, able to buy any firearm he wished, or a market gunner (such hunting was legal in Britain) who had to make every shot count. Neither would have carried a gun that weighed between 11 and 15 pounds unless it gave him a distinct advantage over his handier, more portable 12 or 10. Both types of hunters favored the 8 as the best compromise between power and portability.

And they turned to breechloading 8s very early. Until almost 1960, the English naturalist James Wentworth Day shot a magnum 8 Damascus-barreled double made by Joseph Lang in the late 1870s. (He gave it up when the difficulty of finding 4½- inch brass cartridges for "Roaring Emma," longer than even modern magnum 8s take, became overwhelming.) It shot blackpowder loads of 2½ ounces of shot. By 1910, when William Wellington Greener wrote his famous book *The Gun and Its Development*, magnum 8s were being built with 3¾-inch chambers for three ounces of shot — a formidable load still favored by the hard-core 8-gauge gunner of today.

In Britain, where the 8 is not an outlaw gun, there are still quite a few old ones in use. (The English view the 10 as much as

some do the 16: as a "filler" gauge, though one located between the 12 and the 8 rather than the 12 and the 20.) After World War II, the great English firms of Tolley and Bland*, which specialized in wildfowl guns, went out of business. The better-known gunmakers such as Westley Richards and Holland & Holland suspended work on the expensive-to-make, low-demand wildfowl guns and concentrated on 12-gauges for the more lucrative and aristocratic "game" trade; in England, the sport of duck and goose hunting has always taken a back seat to carefully managed estate shooting.

Still, it wasn't until 1976 that the English cartridge makers decided to discontinue the 8-gauge shell. Ironically, they did so just as a combination of increased farm-feeding goose populations and availability of inexpensive Continental magnum actions triggered a revival of the 8-gauge. Into the gap stepped a few innovative fans of the big bore who either had old guns, or believed that any 8-gauge would kill better than any 10. Alan Myers began to turn out custom brass shells. Douglas McDougall, an East Anglian goose enthusiast who owns two old 8s, began to work up loads based on the Remington "industrial" cartridge, a load first developed not for shooting birds, but for cleaning out boilers. In 1979 he wrote a book, *8-Bore Guns and Loads*, which was so successful that he brought out a sequel, *More 8-Bore Loads*. Soon gunmakers in Spain and Italy began to sell new, inexpensive 8s to the English, guns based on the magnum 10-gauge action that they had previously sold mostly to Americans. Which, whether or not the English knew it at the time, brought the whole big-bore matter full circle.

Eights were once part of the wildfowling scene in America as well as in England. Such famous makers as Lefever and Parker made 8-gauges, Parker at least continuing into the time of fluid steel-barreled guns. In the 1930s, duck populations plummeted drastically, partly because of drought in the prairie states and partly because of the overshooting of the remaining stock. The federal government consequently curtailed shooting

---

* As of this writing, Thomas Bland is back in business under American ownership and is taking orders for custom guns.

and cut down the bag limits. It stopped the shooting of such temporarily endangered species as redheads and canvasbacks and issued the first duck stamp. These were all sensible moves.

But then the Feds began to pass regulations on custom, outlawing such traditional practices as batteries, sinkboxes, live decoys, and big bores. The authorities supposedly asked a small group of wealthy sportsmen what the largest gauge was that they cared to shoot. When most of them answered "the 10," the government banned all larger gauges. Such a move was cosmetic. The issue (then and now) is how many ducks are killed, not which firearm the hunter uses to kill them.

The response from big-bore aficionados had already begun. In 1932, Spencer Olin of the Western Cartridge Company contacted Ithaca with a proposition: If Ithaca would build a gun to hold it, Western would begin production of a new 10-gauge shell. The shell would be 3½-inches long, instead of the mere 2⅞ inches of the then-current Super 10. And it would hold a whopping 8-gauge load of two ounces of shot rather than the Super 10 load of 1⅝ ounces.

The resulting gun and load were not for everyone, but they immediately found a few fans among discerning long-range wildfowlers. The prototype gun, No. 500,000, was almost entirely hand-built in Ithaca's highest grade. It went to Maj. Charles Askins, father of the present-day outdoor writer, and was later passed on to Elmer Keith. Keith, a plain man and a shooter's shooter, was always a booster of the big gun.* The Ithaca, a simple, rugged boxlock with a specially reinforced action, was the perfect gun for the hard-core American wildfowler. It was less expensive than imported guns, and built like a tank. While never as popular as the versatile 12, the Ithaca magnum survived until World War II, when Ithaca phased out its entire double line.

So, why shoot big bores? Are they really that much more efficient than 12s? Well, yes, at least for their particular purposes. Elmer Keith, when asked if a certain caliber wasn't too big for his intended purpose, replied, "You mean it'll kill the game *too dead*?" The anecdote points up one special virtue of the big bore.

*More about this fascinating man later.

51

Although the effective range of the magnum 10 (and the 8, and the 4) can be considerably greater than that of the 3-inch 12 — up to 85 yards, perhaps — most shooters cannot figure leads at this distance. Certainly I can't. But what the big guns will always do is drop such strong birds as ducks and geese dead in the air within normal ranges.

As John Humphrey says in his introduction to Douglas McDougall's book, "Two-and-a-half ounces of number one shot kills stone dead at sixty yards and leaves no cripples." The effectiveness of such loads has to be experienced to be believed; once you know where your gun shoots, your percentage of wounded birds will decrease to almost nothing. At least one anti-10-gauge writer has stated that steel shot cancels the advantage of the big bore. It's hard to see why. Steel shot retains more energy with big pellets, from rarely available in America No. 3s up to BBs. More big pellets fit in a 10 than in a 12. Ballistics expert Tom Roster believes that the 10-gauge shell can be handloaded with steel shot to kill geese at 60 yards — if the shooter is good enough!

In fact, you could make a strong argument for the "re-legalization" of the 8-gauge, and even the mighty 4-gauge, in these times of steel shot requirements. Eight-gauge doubles and singles are currently made in Spain and Italy, proofed for the magnum 8-gauge load of three ounces. Such guns would probably eliminate the crippling associated with steel shot and safely allow 60-yard shots. One Italian maker even offers an immense single 4-gauge in a hammerless modern design that rather resembles a single-barreled trap gun, at least until you pick it up. Then its dimensions become apparent: Its barrel is 46-inches long, it weighs 16½ pounds, and it can handle up to *four ounces* of shot. I should emphasize that all of these guns are built with the expert, long-distance sporting shot in mind. They are not flock-shooting firearms and bear no comparison with the crude "blacksmith's guns" that were used by poachers and market gunners who operated on Chesapeake Bay.

This kind of magnum is at one end of the big-bore spectrum. The hunter who has followed my argument so far should know that shorter, lighter 10-gauge loads — the shells once known as the Super 10 — are still effective. Handloaded with 1⅝ ounces of No. 4 lead pellets, they may be the best duck load around. The amount of shot compares to that in a magnum 12, but the 10-gauge shell produces better patterns and a shorter shot string, perhaps because lower pressures in the bigger bore produce less shot deformation. One West Coast friend handloads No. 6 shot in short 10 shells for long-range, band-tailed pigeon shooting. Though some gunners worry about recoil, the only hard part of his hunt is carrying his 11½-pound Spanish double to the high ridges.

Oh yes, *recoil*. Even some fans of the modern 10 tend to overrate the recoil; one writer called it "dangerous." Actually, the recoil in any well-built 10 is more of a shove, less of a slam, than that of a lighter-weight, 3-inch 12. Even the noise is a sort of a *whummp* that is less bothersome to my ears than the *crack* of some 12s. Only one of the six or so 10s I have owned had unpleasant recoil, and it was not the lightest one. All the others, from massive Spanish doubles, to an autoloader, to a relatively lightweight English Scott, have been as pleasant to shoot as the average wildfowling 12.

And do I take my own advice? Damned right! I've owned any number of magnum 10s and would certainly own an 8 if I had a place to shoot one. I'm looking at a 10-gauge Darne right now. These marsh cannons are, after all, romantic. But they are practical as well, as you will realize the first time you reach out to pull down a snow goose passing at an impossible distance through the gray skies over the Bosque Del Apache, or stop a gale-driven New England black duck dead in the air. Besides, wildfowling itself is romantic. Why else would we freeze in blinds at dawn, study the mysteries of migration, memorize ballistics, or read Nash Buckingham? With a good big bore, you can be part of the grand tradition while equipping yourself with the most efficient, aesthetic, and deadly means to bring down your quarry. The birds deserve no less.

5

Americans from Abroad

One reason that I mention the Ruger as the only possible candidate for modern American classic status is that many recent guns commonly regarded as "American" are made elsewhere. Most of these guns are doubles; labor costs for doubles have traditionally been regarded as too high in post-World War II America, a proposition borne out by the Model 21 if not the Ruger.

The oldest of these foreign-made American guns is not a double, though, but an autoloader, the Belgian-American creation of Utah designer John Moses Browning. American manufacturers were not quick or generous enough with a deal to acquire rights to Browning's shotgun designs. Always a shrewd trader, Browning settled on an arrangement with Belgium's enormous arms corporation *Fabrique Nationale* to make first his autoloader and later his over-under.

The Browning autoloader, produced in Japan today and known as the A5, was first made in 1902; it has certainly stood the test of time. It is beautifully machined of fine steel, rugged to the point of being unbreakable, features decent wood, and, still, a little hand-engraving. It is also a hard kicker, an occasional jammer (as are all autos, without exception) and, above all, one of the least graceful guns ever made. It features a vertical rectangular breech profile, as ugly as a broken back, which makes it very hard to figure vertical alignment; it is flat-sided and front-heavy, and clanks like a steam locomotive as it cycles.

And yet, you can't dismiss it, or Browning's influence. The Sweet Sixteen model, a 16-gauge on a scaled-down frame, was my first gun and I suspect many others'. The old round-knob pistol grip of the Belgian gun, abandoned for awhile along with the sensible dull finish of the older models, was as distinctive in its way as the "eye" on a Parker. The gun has always been good enough to survive, although, like most actions designed before utter uniformity took over, I suspect it is not cheap to produce. It was copied by Remington and Savage between the wars, so that their old humpbacks are also objects of nostalgia. If you can hit with one, don't let me discourage you. Personally, I prefer the round-knob Belgian models and lean to ones without vent ribs. The front-heavy design works better for long-range wildfowling shots than for fast upland shooting, and in such situations, all a vent rib can do is collect saltwater. In recent years, I have recovered my father's old gun to use in sedentary dove hunting; the mild, efficient 16-gauge makes a great dove gun, and the gun's weight mitigates even the light recoil and smoothes my swing.

Browning's other Belgian gun, the "Superposed" over-under double, is both the ancestor of today's most common over-under designs and the subject of a puzzling amount of reverence. Although more hunters probably go afield with such guns than with esoteric side-by-sides, people tend to use what is available. And the availability of Browning-style O/Us probably derives from the same source as that reverence, a historical-economic accident.

Soon after the Second World War, manufacture of all the great American doubles except for the 21 ceased. Labor costs were high, and U.S. shooters, always hooked on "more" and "newer," turned in great numbers to the inexpensive repeater with its promise of extra — if unnecessary — shots. But many still preferred the double gun. Into this gap stepped Browning Arms with its deep-profile, made-in-Belgium over-under. Patented in 1923, it didn't catch on in the U.S. until after the war.

While nobody could call the Superposed a racy gun, it was beautifully made. Checkering and engraving were actually above the old American doubles' standard, especially in their respective lower grades. It could be had in gauges from .410 to magnum 12, including 28, although all gauges from 20 down were based on the chunky 20-gauge frame. It was, according to one friend, "a gunsmith's dream." It sold for a reasonable price. And so Browning's over-under became *the* model for domestic double-gun fanciers throughout the fifties and sixties.

And yet, despite the F.N.'s indubitable high standards, it is hard to see the superposed as an inspired design. Location of the barrels makes for the dumpy profile that still plagues its Japanese and European descendants. The action has a tendency to loosen with age. And I fail to see the necessity for the incredibly complicated forend latch, which must be manipulated in three different directions in order to detach the barrels from the breech — and still doesn't remove the forend from the barrels!

All of which mattered little to a whole generation of shooters, who, if they wanted a quality double, had a choice of an old gun, a Model 21 that cost as much as a car, or the Superposed. When labor problems in Belgium and rampaging inflation sent Superposed prices skyrocketing to levels comparable to the 21's in the early seventies, these shooters turned in droves to the Browning's descendants. These guns, "Citoris" manufactured in Japan by Miroku (Browning) and Olin-Kodensha (Winchester), looked like Browning Superposeds, but were made with considerably less handwork and simpler mechanisms, the second probably an advantage in terms of such features as the forend. These guns, though their prices have risen in turn, still dominate the domestic double-gun market.

They have their virtues, I suppose. They are strong and relatively inexpensive. They are also heavy, glossy, and uninspired; though they are available in small-bore versions, they all use frames no smaller than 20-gauge; the "engraved" models are either acid etched or roll-engraved, rather than cut by hand. (You can tell roll "engraving" easily from handwork: the edges of the cuts done by machine are raised where the metal has been squeezed up and displaced, whereas when the lines have been cut by hand, the pattern is entirely below the surface.) Virtually every model, including the more recently introduced and far more graceful side-by-sides, features a ventilated rib. A ventilated rib is an abomination on anything other than a clay-target gun; it is a locus for dirt, water, and rust to work in and rot your barrels, and is damn-near impossible to clean effectively.

The one exception to the lack of inspiration in these guns was also made by Browning: the BSS "sporter" model, a stout, Japanese-built side-by-side with real virtues. The original side-by-side BSS was a straightforward A&D boxlock with some nice details: bushed firing pins, a decent selective trigger, an attractive wood-to-metal fit, and a pull-down forend latch. But it coupled these features with the fattest beavertail ever seen on a gun, a pistol-grip as hooked as that on a 1950s California custom rifle, and a plastic finish you could see your face in.

The sporter model, introduced a few years later, abandoned all this; by doing so, it became another of the gun world's great bargains. It had a slimmed-down, useful beavertail, an English-style straight grip, and a matte-surfaced stock, all of which, when added to the existing good features of the BSS design and Browning's indisputable good metal, checkering, and finish, added up to a lot of gun for less than $1000. The 20-gauge, which had 3-inch chambers and so conformed to traditional American "all-rounder" standards, was racier and better balanced than the 12. But the 12-gauge might be a good bet in a duck gun for the traditionalist; Japanese Brownings are safe with steel shot.

And the BSS could not be ordered with a ventilated rib.

The best of the Japanese-American guns has had a checkered career, sometimes easy to buy, sometimes unavailable. When Ithaca introduced the SKB line of side-by-sides and overunders in the sixties, they were probably the best shotgun buys in postwar America. Every model was strong, light, and well-balanced; barrels were lined with chrome and plated with dull black chrome rather than conventionally blued on the outside. (While black chrome resembles bluing, it does not rust.) Options ranged from a choice of English-type or gracefully pistol-gripped stocks, choice of forends, and many levels of decoration, to the unusual one of 25-inch barrels perfect for brush work on grouse or wood-cock. Side-by-sides were all simple boxlocks, worthy successors to the NID. The over-unders, also boxlocks, were trim, shallow-framed lightweights with reinforced sidewalls, superficially similar to German Merkels, and could be had in .410 and 28 as well as in the 12- and 20-gauge versions available in side-by-side. (The O/Us did have vented ribs; finding a vertical double without one is about as easy as finding one with two triggers.)

Ithaca SKBs were not without fault, but the faults were entirely superficial; that is, faults of decoration. I do not know why it is so difficult for the Japanese to make an attractive finish for their well-built guns, but it is; the only exception is the Parker Reproduction, which copies old American engraving patterns. Bottom-level SKBs were plain black guns; no fault here. Checkering in all grades was hand cut and of fair quality. The very highest grade target over-unders and field side-by-sides had full coverage, fine-cut scroll engraving, laid on over rather brilliant sil-ver actions, and oil- finished wood. But all the middle grade SKBs had the gaudiest, cheapest, most plastic finishes that ever defaced a fine gun. Everything was silver-gray, acid-etched, white-line-spaced, and high-gloss coated. The wood chosen was not, as you might expect, colorful California claro, but dull low-grade stuff that, in the first years, had fake grain *painted* on!

And yet, well, so what? SKBs were good, very good guns, and — when you can find one — still sell for prices comparable to new pumps and automatics. You can always refinish them, as some friends of mine have, if they offend your eye. A healthy trade mar-ket has sprung up. They handle steel shot. They point more natu-rally than any of the currently popular Japanese over-unders.

Incidentally, two SKB over-under models are now available from Weatherby. The fancier one, with false side-plates, even has screw-in choke tubes. They are of SKB quality, with better wood. The most recent version may be the most handsome reasonably priced over-under on the market, despite Weatherby's old reputa-tion for garishness. Available with either a shallow, rounded semi-pistol grip or a straight hand, it has an oil finish and scroll-engaved side-plates. It is the first gun Weatherby has ever offered that tempts me.

6

England and
the Continent

England is, as has already been mentioned, the source of excel-
lence in shotgun design. The English invented the game gun,
perfected the double, then refined it again and again by a sort
of evolutionary process of elimination until what was left was the
pure essence. The great English guns, doubles made between the
advent of breechloading and the present,* are not only the best
shotguns ever made, but perhaps the most expensive. Prices for
such guns might start at $6,000 in England for an obscure maker or
very plain boxlock from a "name" maker, and range up to — easily
— $50,000. And they cost even more in America.

There are real reasons — that is, reasons not connected to
snobbishness, faddism, or even rampant inflation — for such
prices. The most important is that all the great English guns are
and were handmade.

*Some fanatics would say World War II.

Craftsmen from London and Birmingham patiently shave metal to reveal the graceful shapes, sharp edges, and smooth movements of the classic gun. They black the working faces with smoke, fit them together to see where they make contact, then patiently shave off another ten-thousandth of an inch. The result of such unhurried perfectionism (if you order a London "Best" — the correct term — you will wait at least two years for delivery) is a gun that fits to the precision of one particle of smoke, that will not close if a single cigarette paper is inserted between its faces. English writer Macdonald Hastings says that "...not since the fifth century B.C. has anything been made functionally better than a London Best gun."

I should dispel two myths about England's handmade guns. One is that, because of some foolish sort of inability to change, the makers of Bests do *all* their work by hand...that is, that they do not only the careful fitting, but also the coarse machining by hand, thereby putting themselves at a competitive disadvantage with the innovative gunmakers of, say, Italy. Even Don Zutz says: "...hand labor, costly as it is, can be deemed a waste of time and money when spent on the mere roughing process that advanced machines can do in minutes." He is correct — but he is referring, incorrectly, to the great London makers. Hear Major J.E.M. Ruffer, writing in 1976 about Holland & Holland: "...twenty-five percent of the work is done by machines; the rest is handmade and fitted...where a quarter of an inch of metal has to be removed, it is done (quickly) by a machine. Where only a 'thou' has to be taken off, it is done (more accurately) by hand." These are approximately the same proportions as done in the great Italian shops like Fabbri that Zutz so justly praises. Best guns are Best guns.

Ruffer points up the other heresy about handwork when he says "more accurately." We have become so accustomed to mass production that we assume machines can fit things together or follow a pattern more precisely than the human eye. *This is not true*. On at least two occasions, I have had inexperienced friends say of an inferior job of checkering or metalwork, "Isn't it nice; it's *imperfect* — you can see that it wasn't done by machines." I'm afraid I was not very patient with them. *The human eye and hand* *are capable of more precision than any machine ever built!** To quote Macdonald Hastings again: "...machines can marry two or even three surfaces. The actioners of a Best gun expect to file half-a-dozen parts into a sucking fit."

Wood — French walnut — its quality, aging, choice, and working, is another essential component of the Best, and its expense. The wood that goes into the stock of a Best-quality gun is grown in France or Turkey, cut into blocks, then aged for as many as thirty years before it is carved into the fabulous-figured, graceful stocks that to me are the most beautiful part of a fine gun.

All Best guns are worthy of praise: sidelocks from Purdey, and Powell, and Holland, and Boss; boxlocks from Churchill's and hand-detachable boxlocks from Westley Richards; rare round-actions from Dickson and McKay Brown; guns from such now-defunct makers as Lang, Woodward, Watson, Grant, Blanch, and many, many more. England in its golden age — before the Second World War — probably had more makers of guns than any other country, and most turned out wonderful weapons. At the "merely" good gun level, which includes most guns for colonial use and wildfowl guns from 3-inch 12s to 4-bores, English materials and workmanship are incomparable. At the true "Best" level, English guns (and their Italian and Belgian counterparts) are probably the finest artifacts of the century.

Most of this will make little difference unless you are a lot richer than I am! The proceeds of this book will not buy me a Best-quality gun. Today, prices start around $25,000; selected "golden age" guns may go for considerably more, up into the $50,000 range for vintage Woodwards and Boss "under-overs." If you can afford such a gun, give it the respect it demands and study before you buy. Most British "game" — i.e., upland — guns are chambered for the 2½-inch 12-gauge shell, and to extend the chambers in such a gun against the maker's advice should be a crime. (It *is* illegal in England to sell such a

*Well, all right: a few technically minded readers have reminded me that as of 1994 such accurate machines are now *theoretically* available. They are still too expensive for even the London makers to use.

gun.)   Do not buy a gun that has had the chambers lengthened; if you contemplate such a move yourself, consult with the makers first, or at least with Orvis or Griffin & Howe, who should advise against doing so!   Remember, you can always buy English shells, which will cost an infinitesimal amount of what you pay for the gun and will not wreck it.

If you insist on owning an English gun and are not rich — I'm still searching — you must be prepared to study, shop, study, reject, and learn. Your best bet is the best boxlock you can find, by a less than well-known or defunct maker. There are real bargains here. If you buy by mail, make sure that you have at least a three-day inspection period in which you can return the gun, no questions asked. (I will cover this subject in more detail in the chapter on problems.) If you want a new gun, you will pay more, even for a boxlock. A few makers offer plain-finished but very good-quality boxlocks at prices between $3000 and $5000, and these can be ordered to fit. Well-known names? Be prepared to pay still more. Examine your reasons. If you want a hand-detachable boxlock (droplock) by Westley Richards — a wonderful gun in which the works lift out after you pop open a bottom plate like that on an antique watch, a gun, incidentally, stronger than most boxlocks because of its lack of drill holes through the action; if you want one of the legendary round-action guns from Scotland because you know they are the strongest light guns ever built; if your reasons are scholarly, practical, aesthetic, then by all means save your every penny. If you want a Purdey, not because it is a great gun with a history running back to the time of the Mantons, or because it incorporates and indeed originates most of the patents copied in sidelocks all over the world, but because it is the Rolls-Royce of guns and will impress your friends, save yourself a few bucks and buy a Parker. Your friends will most likely be just as impressed.

I didn't get an English gun last May. I didn't even bring back a photo, or a brochure. All I have left is a business card and a Xerox copy of a manila tag, one that hung from the trigger guard of a plain old boxlock. But now I am surer than ever that somewhere out there is a game gun that I can love and even afford.

Most of my shooting friends assume that the reason one goes to England is to get a gun. (My Magdalena friends consider anything and any reason east of the Rio Grande, including Texas, effete, but that's another story.) But when I finally got to England, I had little time for sport. For one thing, it was spring. Mainly, though, I was there on other business. I needed to travel to Oxford to visit with, and pick the brain of, a friend and correspondent, an African-born scholar who combined the unlikely careers of serious artist and cutting-edge evolutionary biologist.

Somehow even in those surroundings, certain obsessions could surface. Late one rainy night, we sat around looking sleepily at old photographs. The day had been a long one. We had crossed the entire narrow country to visit the Wildfowl Trust and the Falconry Center, then sat down to a North Italian meal prepared by Jonathan's Venetian wife, Elena, and several bottles of wine. Jonathan had entertained us by mimicking, successively: a Victorian colonel; two giraffes in confrontation (one a nervous adolescent, one a truculent old bull); five African servants competing with impressions of five Europeans of different cultures, each mannerism instantly recognizable despite the fact that the entire conversation took place in Swahili; an Australian pedant reading a critical book review in which he recounted the height, width, and thickness of the book in question; an oafish big-game hunter from Alabama; a tame, imprinted forest bird known as a Touraco; and, finally, as a crowning tour-de-force, the wartime BBC broadcast of Churchill's "fight them on the beaches" speech, as heard by a ten-year-old boy in the remotest backlands of Tanganyika, complete with Churchillian grumbles, static, whistles, fades, recoveries, and the plummy tones of the radio announcer. We had laughed until our sides hurt.

Now Jonathan was digging through a stack of old black-and-white snaps, looking, for some reason, for a picture of the Touraco. He flipped one shot of his children aside impatiently. In it, leaning against a tree, was a recognizable English sidelock.

"Nice gun."

"Do you like shotguns? That was my father's. When you get back to London, you ought to go to one of the gun shops. Of course, they're very posh, very pretentious. This was made by what we call a provincial maker — very fine, but only known in a couple of counties."

"Which one?"

"Edwinson Green. I doubt you've ever heard of them in America."

I had to show off. "I *have* heard of them. They once made a three-barreled gun."

Jonathan was amused. "It's a shame that the gun isn't here now. My son Rungwe shoots it these days — he's the hunter of the family." He gazed into the middle distance, remembering who-knows-what. "It has long barrels. For, you know, the very *high* pheasants."

We spoke no more of guns, but Libby and I had a couple of days to kill in London at the end of the trip. I was a little shy of the great "name" shops — not as much because I feared they would treat me rudely, but because I was wary of wasting their time. There was no way short of winning some unlikely lottery that I would ever be able to afford a new London Best; prices were now higher than what my landlady wanted for the house I lived in!

The novelist Thomas McGuane (who shoots a lesser known London Best himself, a Chapman) had suggested that I try Wilkes, where the staff and the gunmakers were the same people, and where I could see the actual workshop and machines. Finally, I was even shyer about that; not only would I waste their time, but I'd take them away from their work. We settled on two establishments: Holland & Holland, because many Americans went there, they had ready-made guns on display (Purdey's, for instance, rarely does), and they had a bookshop; and William Evans. I knew a little about Evans, but another friend had recently bought a wonderful Evans 20-gauge for about $3000, and it seemed that I might inquire about guns there that I could actually afford..

Holland's was, well, Holland's; it did not disappoint, but neither did it give me hope. The staff was polite. But, once it was clear that they weren't going to be fitting either of us for guns, they more or less vanished.

It is clear why Holland does well in a sluggish economy: Apart from guns, they sell clothing, books — atmosphere. They operate an entire store of what we in New Mexico call "yuppie clothes." (Oh, all right, I was wearing my best tweed coat and a tie — when in Rome....) Downstairs is a fine collection of sporting books, both new and out-of-print, where I bought five books for considerably less than a single H&H shooting sweater. And, yes, there are guns. I have never been an enormous fan of Holland & Holland's Royal; Purdeys have nicer details, Boss has incomparably better lines, and I like round actions better than either. But....

On the left as you enter the actual gun shop is a wall of sidelock doubles behind glass, not racked up, but in profile, so you can admire them... 12s, 20s, my beloved 16s. And, yes, they are fine — finer than frog's hair, as David Simpson says. The wood alone was positively erotic. The English double seems to have abandoned its dark stain habit — the red-golds marbled with black veins in the stocks of these Hollands was as lush as anything you ever saw in an Italian gun or an American custom rifle. I'd even dare to say that they have picked up one feature of the Continental gun that I *don't* particularly like: Some of the actions were coin-finished rather than case-hardened.

They started at $28,000 (and I wondered why so cheap.) Look, but don't touch....

At Evans, on St. James Street, we had to buzz them and wait until they opened the door. The atmosphere was darker and, at first, there were fewer guns in evidence. Mr. Bernard Cole, a brisk, short, sandy-haired man, introduced himself. I screwed up my courage and explained that I was a writer, not wealthy, but that if he had any reasonably priced secondhand boxlocks, I'd like to see them, and that I was especially interested in 16s. He motioned us into the back and down the stairs.

I felt that I had arrived at last. The walls were covered with guns, both double game guns, and bolt-action rifles, for Evans probably does more trade in rifles than any other London maker. Opened cases containing fine sidelocks, and matched pairs filled all the horizontal surfaces. Mr. Cole sized me up for a moment, then plucked a boxlock from the walls, opened it, and placed it in my hands.

"It's from our shop. Made in `29. The original owner took it to India. His son brought it in last month. It's mechanically perfect. We'll refinish the stock. And, of course, fit it to you if necessary, at no extra cost. But I think it may fit you pretty well."

I closed it. Raised it cautiously to my shoulder. Swung, dropped it down, raised it a bit faster. The balance was magical. I was mildly amazed. It was a very plain gun, almost without any engraving, and a 12. I thought it might be a colonial-type gun, rather heavy, more like a wildfowl gun or an American double. But it felt like a feather.

"Six pounds? Twenty-eight barrels?"

He almost grinned. "Six-and-a-half, and thirty. Feels all right, doesn't it?"

I couldn't believe it. *"Very* good. I can't believe it's that big."

He showed me several other guns. The only 16 was a lovely best-quality sidelock at £12,000, well above my price range, if significantly below Holland's. I picked an almost identical gun to the first from the rack, and was amazed at its price — £1500. Mr. Cole shook his head minutely. "Not quite as nice. We had to sleeve it." I couldn't even see the joint.

Since I was American, he wanted to show me one other reasonably priced boxlock. "A twenty, very popular in your country." It was a rather odd little gun, with bold game scenes and a high Churchill type rib, although its barrels were a full 28 inches long. I looked at it for a while, trying to like it, but finally shook my head.

"I like the first one." I could almost feel approval radiating off him, although he didn't smile.

The price of the first gun was £1850, within my spoken limits, if beyond what I could get together at the moment. "You realize, I'm a writer. I can't buy it today, but if I'm lucky I might be able to tomorrow."

"That's all right, sir. Let me get you my card. If this one is gone, I'm sure I can find you another one very much like it."

Two days later, on the way out, I rang the buzzer again, wondering if I was being annoying. "I was wondering if I could look at that boxlock twelve again...."

"Certainly, sir. And I made a copy of its tag for you for you to take with you...I thought you might be back. Would you like one for the twenty as well?"

If you visit William Evans Limited, tell Mr. Cole I sent you.

O r, if you want English function and lines and engineering principles but don't care as much about the mystique, you have an enormous range of Continental models ranging in price from much less to a little more than you would pay for a real English gun. With a very few exceptions, most guns from Spain, Belgium, Italy, and France are near copies of English guns built on English patents. (German guns are different and deserve a little space for themselves.)

The Belgian guns of today need take up little time. They are true Best-quality guns, cost just as much as their English counterparts, and may offer a little more latitude in decoration. The Lebeau-Courally sidelocks imported by William Larkin Moore are a good example: The side-by-side is built on Holland patents and starts at $20,000; the over-under, a magnificent version of the English Boss, starts even higher still (more for a 28-gauge). Dumoulin and Forgeron are similar, perhaps a little less expensive. Granger of France, a small shop that makes some of the finest side-by-sides in the world, also makes English-type Bests.

The great Italian guns, including but not limited to Abbiatico and Salvinelli (Famars) Fabbri, and Piotti, are also mostly built on English patents. Again, they are handmade and very expensive. The Italians (a little ethnic pride here) are more innovative in finish and detail than the other Best makers. They employ engravers in a wide range of styles, from carved baroque that would not have looked out of place in Renaissance Florence, to "bulino" or bank-note engraving, a process by which a pattern of dots is built up with a hand tool to give an almost photographic image.

Italian makers are more likely to be innovative in other external, though not fundamental, ways. Famars in particular has created guns that are startling without abandoning classic principles. They have revived the hammer gun, often with flaring fences that contrast with the simple lean lines of the rest of the gun. They have built a four-barreled 28-gauge that still manages to look trim. They have even built guns without engraving, the better to set off the subtle lines and perfect wood. All these guns are probably as fine as any English Best (some dare claim that Fabbris are better, at least for competition guns) and may well be more decorative.

Inexpensive Italian guns are more common in England than America, the only exception being Bernardelli, which has several American outlets and also builds higher-quality guns. The inexpensive ones are generally built on English lines, though heavier, and tend toward rather bright coin-finished receivers and brilliantly polished, high-luster-blued barrels. They are strong, and have a reputation for good materials and dubious single triggers. Aesthetically, they are pretty unexciting.

One Italian maker, the world's oldest gunmaker in continual production, bridges the gap between the Ferrari-class guns at the pinnacle of Italian gunmaking, and the low-cost, conventional production models. Beretta makes an enormous variety of shotguns that range from inexpensive but extremely well thought-out, trim boxlock over-unders, to Best-quality sidelocks at ten times the cost. The less expensive models are in the best-buy category.

Beretta's side-by-sides are conventional, their over-unders are bolted on the sides of the barrels rather than on the Browning plan* and so are slender without sacrificing strength. The boxlocks, which can be ordered new for as little as $1100, use two cones projecting from the standing breech to hold down the barrels. The more expensive sidelocks use a slightly more complicated system, with crossbolts in the action working against lugs on the face of the barrels.

These Beretta back-action sidelocks are *not* built on English patents and are both innovative and simple. The "bridle" employed in all other sidelocks, the part that holds all the moving parts against the lockplate like the top of a sandwich, is integral with the lockplate. This makes for both a reduction of the number of moving parts and great strength. The insides of the locks are engine-turned — polished with a dappled surface — and in the highest grades, gold-plated against rust** as in the finest English Bests. The outsides are handsomely engraved with Italian floral designs.

Until recently these "SO" series Berettas were reasonably priced. They now range from $10,000 to $28,000, still lower than what many competitors cost. Every so often one shows up at a bargain price in the used-gun ads. You could do worse than to grab it.

Italy also builds the world's best target guns. Such names as Perazzi and Marocchi are justly famous, and in recent years have built a few high-priced field guns as well, mostly shallow framed over-unders. But since almost all their guns are used for competition rather than hunting, they are rather outside the scope of this book.

G erman guns are beautifully made and look like cuckoo clocks. Having made this gross generalization, I want to retract it, or at least qualify it.

*I should mention that a slim profile on an over-under is not "merely" aesthetically superior; such guns drop the barrels into the leading hand and so point better.

**This hidden gold is one of the subtlest signs of a great gun. It is sometimes visible on the exposed parts of the ejector mechanism in the firearm.

Certainly there are many German (and Austrian) guns, especially ones made for foreign customers, that are as subtly decorated as any other fine gun. But German guns made for the local trade tend to have ornate game scenes (the turkey-sized *auerhahn* grouse, wild boar, and roe deer are most popular, along with packs of medieval-looking hounds) surrounded by oak leaves on the metal, in turn surrounded by basket-weave checkering or carved fish scales on the grip, which are *again* surrounded by acorns or carved oak foliage spreading out into the stock. Add a staghorn (or in modern times, sadly, plastic) trigger guard, a cheek-piece (perhaps with decorative carving around the edges), a high-mounted detachable scope (for the German sportsman will likely have a rifle barrel mounted below his shotgun barrels), a hooked pistol grip, and perhaps, still, exposed hammers, and you have a handmade "drilling," an engineering marvel that looks like — well, a cuckoo clock.

I sort of love such guns, which probably exhibit more hand-fitting than anything else built by man. But you have to admit they exhibit an aesthetic ideal far from that of the lean-limbed British Best. Good pre-war drillings feature fine wood and incredible engraving and may be extremely useful guns. The shotgun barrels are usually 16-gauge; the rifle either 7 or 8mm x 57 rimmed (still available) or 9.3mm's of various lengths, again, mostly still available. They are also, amazingly, quite light. Their main drawback is that they are so full of tiny interdependent moving parts that once one breaks, you may have to fix a chain reaction of nagging problems. Try to get one that already works. And if you can find one that has been made for an American, in .30/06 or .30/30, you will have a gem.

Makers are almost immaterial — there once must have been literally hundreds, and they all made good guns. The best I ever saw was a sidelock 16 x 16 over .30/30 hammerless, made by the well-known firm of Sauer for an American. It had white-tailed deer engraved on the locks!

Avoid postwar models. All are expensive, most are too heavy, and some have plastic trigger guards. A lot of old ones came over in the hands of GIs after the war. If they haven't been butchered, such guns make interesting restoration projects. Go slowly.

A ll German guns share some properties with the drillings. Germans seem far more conscious of and impressed by bolting devices than the English. Virtually every German gun has, as a minimum, the cylindrical sliding "Greener" crossbolt common on English wildfowl and pigeon guns and double rifles. Most also have "side clips" — little curving wings of metal projecting forward from the sides of the standing breech. To reinforce the angle of the breech, many have a limb of reinforced metal protruding like a swollen lip at the outside edge of the breech. Such additions may make the gun safer; they certainly make it heavier.

German and Austrian over-unders add the ultimate bolt, the Kersten, a modified Greener that goes through *two* rib extensions. It must inevitably add weight and complication. And yet the best German gun, and perhaps one of the world's finest shotguns, is a deep-framed, under-lugged, over-under that incorporates both a reinforced breech and the Kersten fastener, yet manages to be lively and fast-pointing despite the fact that it breaks all the rules.

The Merkel is a distinctive-looking gun. In addition to its formidable profile, it uses a unique forend made of three pieces of wood. The top pieces are bolted to the barrels, which they cover to a higher point than on other guns; the lower piece, which is very thin, comes off. The result is that your forward hand wraps around the barrels, a sure aid to fast pointing. The frame of the Merkel is deep and seemingly surrounded by bolts and reinforcements, but these safety measures give the maker the confidence to remove unnecessary metal. The result is a frame that is lighter than it looks. The barrels, made these days of steel so hard that they are guaranteed for use with steel shot, are slim and light. The stocks, at least on the export models, are as trim as those of any classic game gun. The whole gun seems to taper away at the ends, placing the center of balance, the deep-framed action, squarely between your hands.

One of the few guns I really miss is a Merkel 12-gauge made in 1956. It had 30-inch barrels, weighed 7 pounds, and handled better than most 6-pound American guns with 26-inch barrels. The same model is still imported today. It comes in all gauges but 10, and, despite the fact that its exterior finish isn't what it used to be, may still be one of the best gun bargains of our time.

Sidelock Merkels are even better, though vastly more expensive. They feature all the Merkel goodies, plus hand-detachable locks, even more bolting (!) and fabulous engraving and wood.

Although there are many interesting (and often nameless) "guild" guns from the Continent that you'll see from time to time in shops and at gun shows, there is one line of sleepers that you should watch for: Sauer boxlocks made from the mid-twenties up until WW II. If you find one of these with a scalloped joint between the action and wood and sideclips on the fences, look it over very carefully. These guns often have rather plain, dark wood (or wood darkened by age) and may have only a modest amount of engraving. But they are among the finest boxlocks available, with glass-smooth barrels, intercepting safety sears, and interior parts polished like those of fine watches. They include English-type 16s and upland 12s, as well as magnum duck guns, some with made-as-3-inch chambers. They are rarely heavily Germanic in decoration. I picked up a big 12 — it weighs 8 pounds, on a magnum action — a few years back for very little. It is as nice as an English Greener.

All modern double shotgun but one are built on the "break-action" principle; they pivot at the angle of the action and the barrels. This is an effective and simple system, one that seems so natural that most people think that it is the only way for a double to open. It may come as a surprise that since about 1890, in France, a company called Darne (*not* pronounced "Darnay") has built elegant side-by-sides on a frame as rigid as that of a muzzle-loader.

The barrels do not drop down as in a conventional break-action double, but remain fixed while the standing breech slides back to load or to eject spent shells. You open the breech by means of a lever that fits flush into the back of the breech itself, giving the Darne a uniquely sleek profile broken only by two small tabs or "ears" that you grasp between thumb and forefinger. The action is not merely aesthetic but also very strong, as it eliminates the weakest point of the conventional double, the hinge pin. Old Darnes don't get loose; they just get smoother.

But the sliding breech is not the only unique feature of the Darne. In a side-by-side double, the barrels must converge slightly. Since the standing breech is a flat surface, the base of the shell can only contact it at one point. Every time you shoot, the shell moves backward some fraction of an inch and slams into the breech. Despite the fact that this distance is measured in thousandths of an inch, this "slam" is alleged to be a serious factor in recoil. But in the Darne, the sliding breech is equipped with so-called "obturator discs" at the breech end, each at right angles to the axis of its bore. These disks slightly resize the rim of the shell as the breech is closed, entirely preventing "secondary recoil."

The final innovation of the Darne-patent gun is its rib. Darnes have a single rib only, rather than an upper and lower rib joining the barrels. Although Darnes were made with conventional-profile ribs, the classic choice of one of these guns is the "swamped" rib, which plunges from the breech down to a level between the barrels, emerging at a more conventional height at the muzzle.

All Darnes featured world-class wood-to-metal fit — looking as though the wood grew around the metal — hinged front triggers, and amazing lightness without a corresponding increase in recoil. They had two small faults: the mildly inconvenient side safety, inevitable since the action lever occupies the usual place for a safety slide, and the fact that it takes a moment to remove the breech, making it a slower process to look down the barrels than in a break-action double. But these are quibbles. Not only were Darnes strong and beautiful, they were incredibly natural to use. To shoot something with a Darne resembled pointing your finger at the target and watching it disintegrate.

You will notice that I have been speaking in the past tense; to the dismay of the world's hard-core Darne fans, the company went bankrupt in the early seventies. We watched as prices for used guns, especially the slender 20s and 28s, soared into the middle thousands from their production-years' costs of $300 to $700.

In 1985, a query to gun writer Roger Barlow brought me the news that the Darne had been revived under the name of Bruchet. Paul Bruchet, a former employee of the original firm, has bought all the original machinery and, with the help of his son and an engraver, hopes to turn out at least 100 guns a year. Cost is higher than in the early days, from a little over $3,000 for a plain model, to more than $8,000 for one of the true Best gun quality. But such prices are still bargains for a handmade gun of such originality and elegance.

A ll of the guns dealt with in this chapter have been expensive. Are there any real bargains in fine European doubles? I'd answer with a qualified "yes." There are two areas you should consider. One is a group of obscure guns of Belgian make from between the wars. Some resemble English guns, others tend to the Greener bolts and cheekpieces of the German boxlocks. There are many names available; you have to shop around. Francottes may be too well-known. Neumanns are often delightful and cheaper. I once owned a sidelock, a George Simonis from about 1920, that was indistinguishable from an English gun. It had gold inside the locks, marble-cake wood, fine detailing, and no reinforcements or Greener bolts. You wouldn't believe how little it had cost me. *Shop around.*

The other area, perhaps more congenial if you want a new gun, a small bore, or English styling, is that of the better Spanish guns. There is a lot of pernicious nonsense circulating about Spanish guns. They are alleged to be soft-metaled, crude, "season guns" (that is, you shoot them for a season and they fall apart). Maybe, just maybe, this was partially true twenty years ago — though gun writing godfather Jack O'Connor shot two AyAs and an Arrizabalaga for years and had no complaints beyond occasional and curable single-trigger malfunctions. It is most emphatically not true today. Some writers have complained about Spanish guns "copying" English guns. Apart from the fact that nobody complains about $24,000 copies, only affordable ones, you might remember that one reason that the Spanish makers do guns in the English style is that England is their biggest market. AyA — Aguirre y Arranzabal — became England's best-selling maker! The relevance of this phenomenon to durability is that the English shoot more shells per year than we do — often thousands every season. AyAs and other quality Spanish guns stand up to this pounding with no malfunction.

Every time a writer sits down to make statements about Spanish guns — what is available from whom, how much it costs, what models exist — he risks being out of date by the time his work is published. The situation seems to be stabilizing at the moment, but I've said that before. Here's a partial report from early 1994; I make no guarantee that it will be true by September!

Arrieta, which confines itself to high-grade guns, makes among other models a 28-bore that several knowledgeable friends prize. My publisher, Chuck Johnson, shoots a "made-as" left-handed sidelock Arrieta in 12. It has a reversed lever and trigger guard, and cast-on (cast-off for a lefty) stock. It is one of the nicest Spanish guns I know.

Garbi makes a bewlidering variety of fine, rather expensive sidelocks, including some that are guaranteed for steel shot. William Larkin Moore of Westlake Village, California, is their major importer.

Arrizabalaga. This maker specializes in best-quality side-locks. Like Purdey, he makes only one grade of guns. They are not cheap, nor do they come quickly. The ones I've seen are worth the wait.

Both Orvis and Dunn's carry several grades of customer sidelocks from Spain, including beautiful, rounded-edge (*not*, "round-action") models. Both have gone to several makers, but the Orvis and Dunn's names guarantee quality.

There are cheaper Spanish guns around, but I'd be cautious. I can vouch for the makers mentioned above.

7

Rifles

Europeans dominate the field in shotguns. Americans make the best rifles. There are many reasons for this, rooted in history and the nature of the terrain. Perhaps the most important are that there are far more opportunities for the non-millionaire American to hunt with a rifle than there are for his English or German counterparts; and, second, that a good single-barreled rifle is far more amenable to mass-production and machining than a double-barreled anything.* Which is why this chapter will ignore the fine European double rifle, made for the wealthy on reinforced shotgun actions and basically mechanically identical to any given firm's shotguns.

First, let me define rifle. A rifle is a long arm in which the bore contains cut grooves or "rifling" that spiral from the chamber to the muzzle of the barrel. These grooves and "lands," or raised

*Double barrels must be "regulated" by hand to shoot to the same spot, a process that may take hundreds of shots. Side-by-sides are harder to regulate than O/Us.

portions, impart an axial spin to the metal bullet, stabilizing its flight and aiding its accuracy. Strictly speaking, rifles are not "guns" — only smoothbores such as muskets and shotguns deserve this definition. But despite the army's rhyme ("This is my rifle, this is my gun...") such distinctions are usually considered pedantic today.

Before we consider individual rifle makers, we must deal with the matter of caliber. Strictly speaking, caliber is merely the diameter of the bore. But though shotguns use a standardized, if archaic, measurement, the naming of rifle calibers can be maddeningly arbitrary. Calibers can be expressed in fractions of inches or in millimeters, can incorporate years of introduction, black-powder equivalents, rounded-off numbers, manufacturer's or inventor's names, and even *nicknames.*

I am not exaggerating. First consider the old standby American .30/06—a "thirty" (³/₁₀ inch) caliber introduced in 1906. Next, the 7mm Mauser, perhaps better known as the 7 x ("by") 57, 57 being the case length in millimeters, which is how the ultra-rational Germans designate all cartridges. (Mauser was the cartridge's first maker; .30/06s are sometimes called .30/06 *Springfields* for the same reason.) How about the .45/70 government ("government" because it was used in military rifles in the 19th century), a .45-caliber cartridge that once used 70 grains of black powder? Don't attempt to load it with 70 grains of smokeless! Or a .30/30, a "thirty" (I'll get to those quote marks) that was first loaded with 30 grains of smokeless powder? Next, consider "rounded-off numbers": the .30/06 actually has a bullet diameter of .308 inches. But don't call it a .308; that designation is reserved for a shorter modern cartridge. (You could call it a 7.62 x 63mm, though....) Manufacturers' names? Try 7mm Remington. Inventors? .257 Roberts. Nicknames? .22 Hornet or .220 Swift.

Personally, I think all this business is fun; American caliber designations have more soul and history than the perfectly rational German system. But you will simply have to learn, and memorize, caliber data; there is no shortcut. Tables published in the yearly *Gun Digest* and by some ammunition manufacturers can help. They arrange cartridges by bullet diameter rather than by power; a small bullet can have a large brass case full of powder behind it, giving it much more energy than a larger bullet backed by less powder. The ballistic figures in these tables, which also include bullet drop at various ranges, velocity, and energy, will soon begin to make sense.

On calibers I am an extreme moderate and an ultra-traditionalist. Nowadays, an enormous range of calibers is available, with a strong trend toward fast bullets and flat trajectories; also, contrarily, toward what I would call "lite" (as in "lite beer") calibers alleged to give traditional results in shorter cartridges, which in turn are used in lighter rifles. Examples of the first are Weatherby's "proprietary" calibers and most modern varmint cartridges; of the second, the .308 (substituting for the .30/06) and the 7mm/08 (a .308 with a 7mm bullet stuck in it).

The first category may have its uses; my most experienced big-game hunting friend, Tom McIntyre, is very fond of the ultra-flat shooting, ultra-long-range, ultra-noisy and hard-recoiling Weatherby cartridges. But consider your needs. If you go on twelve guided big-game hunts a year, often in far-off places, and must shoot when the guide tells you to or risk having no other shot even if the game is far away; if you are built to handle recoil; above all, if you shoot often enough that you know that you can place all your shots accurately with such a weapon, then by all means shoot a Weatherby caliber. (I still don't like the actual rifles much.) Tom is one of the most dedicated and knowledgeable hunters I know, goes on such trips, and shoots constantly between them. Very few other hunters I know shoot such rifles well.

Most "lite" cartridges are simply superfluous; they are designed to work in "lite" rifles, which are also unnecessary. I am a fan of featherweight shotguns, but a rifle can be *too* light. Try to hold a 6-pound rifle on target. These 18-inch-barrel, toothpick-profile jobs are a fad; they, and their associated cartridges, will fade, while the great old ones will go on forever.

Let me say something outrageous: With the possible exception of the .22, which is a separate kind of cartridge used for rather different purposes, *caliber does not matter.*

I'll leave you in shock for a moment to deal with .22s. The .22 is best known in America as a "first" rifle. Because .22s are quiet and accurate and have no perceptible recoil, they are a good choice for the beginner, as well as for the target shooter. They are "rimfires"— their strikers are arranged to hit the rim of the cartridge, which is crimped full of an explosive material that in turn ignites the powder that propels the bullet. The tiny, soft bullets do not achieve the velocity of those from larger rifles. (Which is not to say that they are not dangerous; they are true rifles and under the wrong circumstances they can kill humans at long distances.) Because .22s attain low velocities and use soft-lead bullets, their barrels are often made of softer metal than those of other rifles.

For hunting, .22s are mainly useful on squirrels. You cannot kill either a turkey or a woodchuck consistently with a .22, or even with its longer-cased, higher velocity, but otherwise identical cousin, the ".22 magnum" or (properly) .22 Winchester Rimfire Magnum. For such animals you need a .22 Hornet, which shoots heavier, better-constructed bullets.

The great caliber debates are prefigured in the writings of two men. This century has seen many so-called outdoor writers come and go. Some have been adventurers, some "experts," some literary, and some painfully down-home. Some are already mercifully forgotten; a few will always be read. But I doubt that any two writers (or for that matter any one writer) will ever again have the influence and following that Jack O'Connor and Elmer Keith gained in the forties and wielded through the sixties. And though we have gained more sophistication, we may have given up a little of the robust flavor of that more innocent time.

Though they were both Westerners, they couldn't have been more different. O'Connor, born in Arizona, was an educated man, a journalism professor and a novelist who always cultivated a gentleman's image. He wore three-piece suits in civilization, and his trademark Borsalino hats brought some of that same elegance even to the field. He was literate, sardonic, and understated, and probably the only so-called gun writer to get a *New York Times* obituary.

Elmer was born in Missouri and grew up as a working cowboy in the mountain West. He worked as a big game guide (O'Connor in later life mostly *hired* guides). Instead of O'Connor's rakish fedoras, Elmer (one doesn't somehow think of O'Connor as "Jack" in the same way) sported enormous ten-gallon hats out of a

1920s western. He usually added a cigar and at least one six-shooter to the ensemble. If O'Connor ever shot a handgun, I can't remember his recording the fact.

As any reader of the two knows, their prejudices and differences in style did not just extend to their ideas about rifles — they were embodied in them. O'Connor favored modest, rational, flat-shooting calibers embedded in elegant, classic stocks. He popularized and defended the .270 and was also fond of the .30/06 and the 7 mm Mauser.

Elmer, on the other hand, demanded and eventually got the .44 magnum handgun cartridge, shot a 10-gauge magnum double at geese all his life, and loved anything above .338 caliber — fans and detractors alike might say, the higher above, the better. He liked .45/70s, anything with the name "magnum," and all the elephant calibers. He might have had the most complete collection of fine English double and single rifles of any man of modest means alive in his time. He at least once strongly implied that the .30/06 wasn't good for *anything*.

Oddly, except for such occasional bouts of rhetorical excess on Elmer's part, both O'Connor and Keith wrote far more sense than nonsense. They did take occasional potshots at each other (without mentioning names), but this might just have been good business. In his outspoken, posthumous *The Last Book* (Amwell Press), O'Connor wryly calls Elmer "more knave than fool." Their "followers" could occasionally get carried away. O'Connor's fans were likely to sneer condescendingly at Elmer's style, but Elmer's fans... well, here's another quote from *The Last Book*, from the chapter "Big Bore Boys":

> "...users of big bores always attack the users of small bores...The big bore boys also feel that anyone who doesn't enjoy getting belted out from under his hat by a hard-kicking rifle is not very masculine, if not actually gay."

O'Connor's writing was incomparably more elegant than Elmer's, though he wrote so many books, it could become repetitive. He also wrote a memoir, *Horse and Buggy Days*, and two novels, *Boomtown* (made into a movie starring Clark Gable) and

Conquest. Elmer wrote an autobiography, first called simply *Keith*, then released in an expanded version more aptly titled *Hell, I Was There!* It is exuberant and utterly outspoken, something O'Connor never achieved until *The Last Book*.

O'Connor never stopped growing intellectually — in his introduction to the 1984 Amwell reprint to his classic Derrydale *Game in the Desert*, he could apologize for his anti-mountain lion ("I for one will not regret their passing") attitude of the thirties, while Elmer advocated shooting predators, including eagles and hawks, until the end of his life.

And yet, and yet...without in any way running down O'Connor — who was the one I grew up on, and whose style is closer to my own — I find that the older, more experienced, and just possibly more Western I get, the more I appreciate Elmer. Part of it is simply getting to know the kind of blunt, honest, plain-spoken Westerners ("Hell, I was there!") that he was; part is meeting some of the many fine hunters and writers he befriended in their youth. But part is a sort of ballistic sophistication, the recognition that, day-in, day-out, if you hunt *a lot,* a big, slow bullet will probably work more consistently than a small, fast one. *If you can handle it*, it will work better than anything. Remember, Elmer was alleged to have asked about a "too-large" caliber: "You mean it'll kill *too dead*?"

Call this the neo-Keithian school if you will; present day proponents include Ross Seyfried, who may have shot more legitimate game than anyone in our generation and who is as sophisticated as O'Connor; and *Sports Afield's* Tom McIntyre, as elegant a prose stylist as exists in sporting letters, who states in *The Way of the Hunter* that, "I am more of a Keithian than an O'Connorite."

Think of Elmer as a straight shot of sour-mash bourbon and O'Connor as silky-smooth Irish whiskey, and you'll have it about right. Both writers ended up in Idaho's Snake River Country, and by most accounts they got along. It doesn't take too much imagination to see them together in some hunter's Valhalla, still deafening each other with shots of their happy conflict.

So what does this have to do with whether caliber matters? Quite a bit, at least in simplifying them. *Of course*, the difference between a huge, powerful, slow rifle caliber such as a

.458 Winchester magnum and a flat-shooting, speedy little varmint round like the .22/250 matters. You wouldn't shoot an elephant with the latter, nor a woodchuck with the former. But I submit that within each broad category (of which there are three or, at most, four), the majority of practical differences are minimal — or, to put it less politely, are mostly a gun writer's way of making an easy living.

I admit this is a heretical notion. From the golden-oldie days of O'Connor versus Keith, differences between .270 inches and .308, between case lengths of 57mm and 63, have been discussed seriously. The real hard-core magazines of the gun fanciers still present titles like "7mm Versus .30/06: The Experts' Opinions," as though it's an issue of real import. There are perhaps some beneficial results: The beginner can learn a lot about ballistics and history from such articles. But apart from boring readers to death, these debates can cause a real problem. They can seriously confuse the beginning hunter and make even the experienced field shooter lose confidence in arms that are a lot better than adequate. It's human nature to be dissatisfied, and it doesn't matter that old Johnny B. has shot thirty bucks with his ancient Remington thirty-ought: When Col. Chuck Magnum writes in *American Gunner* that the .30/06 is an obsolete caliber and good only for sissies, John is going to have some doubts.

He shouldn't; experience should tell him this much. But since it is mostly the followers of my profession who have reduced him to this sorry state, I'm going to rectify it. Let me be clear: Most likely if you have a rifle with which you have killed deer, you should shoot it in perfect confidence. You should check its sights at the very least before every hunting season, not just on an old can at a paced 100 yards, but on formal targets at measured distances. You *should* be aware of your caliber's range limitations and of the possible effect on drop of different bullet weights within the caliber on the long side of the range. You *should* shoot as often as possible, in season and out, at benches, offhand, sitting, from rests, and from the kind of awkward stances that you often must take afield. You owe it to the game to shoot very well, whatever caliber you choose. Other than that, all you need is confidence.

But maybe you still don't believe me. Maybe the gun-writing brethren have you hypnotized. Would the fact that the single-most experienced hunter of Western big game that I know, a man who has hunted every species in the Lower 48 but sheep and puts most in the freezer every year, uses only a .30/06 and a .243 make a difference to you?

No? I thought not. This business is insidious and deep-seated. So let's get analytical rather than merely give examples.

First, consider the American quarry for your centerfire rifle. (Rimfires —.22s and .22 magnums — are another issue; those who use them for game larger than squirrels are either poachers or stupid or both.) You have "varmints" — a broad and unbiological term covering animals that are considered pests, including many rodents and unrelated small predators. One thing they all have in common is that they weigh less than forty pounds. Next you have, well, let's call it "deer," though it includes animals from the tiny javelina up to ones the size of, though arbitrarily not including, elk. Finally, you have truly big game. In North America this category includes only the moose, elk, and the grizzly.

Now, I am not rash enough to argue that one rifle would cover all these alternatives. Although, if you only shoot varmints for pest control, and so do not have the problem of many rather heavy-recoiling shots in close succession, and if you only take sure, long-range shots on the "big three," you could well get along with one, a 7x57 or .270 or .30/06. What I'm saying is that you will need only three, at absolute most. And that which you pick within each of these already slight arbitrary categories has more to do with what's available or what appeals to your eye or what your favorite gun writer shoots than with ballistics.

This is particularly true of the great middle ground, the "deer" rifle calibers. While some of the older cartridges such as the .30/30 sport rainbow trajectories that will force you to stalk closer than if you are using a .270, all the popular deer cartridges will kill deer.

Here in New Mexico, I know one-rifle hunters who use the .243, .250/3000. .257 Roberts, various 6mms, .35 Remington (in the West!), .270, 7mm, .30/06, an old .303 Enfield military rifle, and the .308. They hunt mule deer, pronghorn, elk, and occasional exotics.

Any one hunter does about as well as any other, and few if any ever lose a wounded animal. Of course, the .270 boys may chance longer shots. But in the real world, I don't know that it matters much. My bird-hunting partner takes all of the above with a .58-caliber muzzleloader, a firearm with a practical range half that of a .30/30!

Some people will not believe that the old-time calibers will still harvest game. Whether these same people believe that the earth is a flat disc resting upon a giant turtle is an open question. O'Connor says in *The Last Book*:

> "The thesis of about half [Keith's] stuff is that only heavy bullets of large caliber kill game well. If Elmer has ever told us just why lighter bullets of smaller caliber fail to kill, I have never run across it. For my part, I have made some irreverent wise-cracks about this neglect. What happens?...Do the bullets bounce off? Do they vanish in a puff of smoke when they hit elk hair? Do they blow up on the surface?...Elmer has apparently found that animals get away wounded because hunters use 'inadequate' calibers on them. It is my own experience that animals get away wounded because careless and unskillful hunters do not place shots well."

Of course, one might take the "one gun" thesis too far. Where it begins to break down a little is at the extremes, when you apply it to small-bore, long-range varmint calibers such as the .220 Swift and the .22/250, and to elephant calibers. If you spend a lot of time shooting at prairie dogs a quarter of a mile away (I don't), you will need every advantage in range and flat trajectory that you can get. You will also need quality barrels and expensive optics. Here, minutiae begin to count. You must balance the long-range resistance to crosswinds of heavier calibers such as the .25/06 against their heavier cumulative blast and recoil. All of this can be fascinating. Whether it is hunting at all, in the primal sense of out-witting animals, is a totally different question; some varminters out here shoot prairie dogs from the hood of a 4WD, with lunch on the side.

And as far as heavy calibers go, their value when you are going after animals that "run both ways" is unquestionable. You can certainly kill a distant grizzly, one that is unconscious of your presence, with a .270 or .30/06; you might not even slow down the same bear, if it charges, with anything less than a .375. But although elk are tough enough to run a long way when shot a little off-center with a "small" caliber, I suspect that more are killed with .270s and .30-oughts than with anything else. They are the calibers that hunters use. Besides, you will see all sorts of eccentrics who do succeed with odd calibers because they are hunters. I know a crackpot who shoots whitetails back East with a loaded-down .458; as Elmer said, you can't kill them *too* dead, and the slow bullets don't tear up the meat.

On the other extreme, I know a hunter, a rancher with a fair amount of land backing up against the mountains, who has scored three successive one-shot kills on elk with a .22/250. (I don't recommend it, unless your land houses a herd of unwary elk and you are a precision shot addict who is willing to pass up fifty poor shots for one golden opportunity; hell, I *still* don't recommend it.) The famous W.D.M. "Karamojo" Bell did kill hundreds of elephants with a 7x57 and quite a few Scottish stags with a .220 Swift. Ireland, for complicated political reasons, bans private ownership of virtually all adequate deer calibers, allowing only .22/250 and 5.6mm Mannlicher, and Irish hunters do very well with these puny loads. Still, it's well to remember that Robert Ruark coined his famous phrase "use enough gun" after wounding several small antelope with a .220. Even hunting ability does not make up for lack of common sense.

Calibers will continue to proliferate as new hunters start up and old ones, being normal human beings, keep looking for an advantage that is also a shortcut. The hardest thing for any hunter, or any person, to learn is that there are no shortcuts.

I could be happy forever if the only calibers in existence were, say the .250/3000 or .257 Roberts on the light end, the .30/06 and 7x57 in the middle, and the .375 and almost any British propri-etary elephant double big bore — say the .470 or the .416 — on the big end. All of these calibers are more than a half-century old.

These are all balanced, moderate (well all but the .4s!), golden mean-type loads. They offer moderate velocity, deep penetration, good accuracy, and a history of proven kills. Let me describe a few favorites in detail, small to large.

The .250/3000 is a cartridge that uses bullets of .25 inches (actually .257) and was once thought to have factory ballistics of 3000 feet per second (it didn't). It is also called the .250 Savage, for its original manufacturer. It was chambered in the wonderful Savage Model 99, and I believe that the combination still makes the best light deer rifle ever invented. You can also find it in some bolt-action rifles. It is a deadly killer with no recoil to speak of, a little more limited in range than some of the larger cartridges. (Stalk closer.)

The 7x57, originally a turn-of-the-century German military cartridge, is probably the lightest recoiling "all-around" rifle in existence. It is great for deer, and has been used, as I said, by the legendary Karamojo Bell for elephants. Other fans included Jim Corbett, who used it on tigers, and Jack O'Connor, who liked it for sheep. It is probably the smallest rifle one should consider for very large game, and even then, elephants are a bit much. Factory loads (as opposed to hand, or as the English more appropriately say, "home" loads) include a deep penetrating, 175-grain bullet suitable for black bear and (maybe) elk, and a 139-grain job useful for open-country deer. Handloading makes it even more versatile. If I had to pick one rifle, it would be a 7mm Mauser.

The .30/06 and .270 are two very similar descendants of the 7x57, both with longer cases and more power. The .30/06 has a greater bullet diameter than the 7mm (7mm is .284 inches); the .270, obviously, slightly less. They make a little more bang and recoil than the old Mauser. The .30/06 shoots heavier bullets, theoretically enabling you to kill larger animals faster. The .270 shoots a little flatter, theoretically enabling you to kill animals farther away. They're both great; you probably need only one of them, and the real-world ballistic advantage of either over the 7x57 is probably imaginary. The .30/06 is available in a wider range of factory loadings, and in more stores, than any other rifle caliber.

The .375 Holland & Holland Magnum is a long cartridge shooting a heavy, medium-diameter bullet invented by the great English gunmaker to provide a round suitable for *anything* encountered by the wealthy, peripatetic English sportsmen of the turn of the century. Jack O'Connor called it "the world's most useful cartridge." It is much smaller than the heavy, slow elephant cartridges of .4 to .6 calibers popular then (though it packs nearly as much energy). It is not as flat-shooting as a .270 (though in its lighter loadings it does approach the ballistics of the .30/06), but shoots flat enough and "slowly" enough to use on red deer and, in America, elk. That "slowly"—relative in any case — may require a little explanation. A Weatherby, say, can jelly meat for six inches around the bullet hole. The "slow" .375 just sort of bores on through. Really slow cartridges like the .45/70 also are kind to meat, but have rainbow trajectories that make them less than useful at long ranges.

The .375 H&H does recoil; anything that has 4263 foot pounds of energy at the muzzle, as opposed to, for instance, 2313 in the 7mm Mauser, is bound to. But, in its proper, moderately heavy, long-barreled form, it is probably the heaviest caliber that is comfortable for the mythical average shooter. I am no Tom McIntyre. I am moderately recoil-sensitive and still don't mind the .375. I'd rather go to the dentist than shoot one of McIntyre's Weatherbys.

And one more caution here: Do not confuse the .375 H&H with the uninteresting so-called big-bore .375 Winchester of the 1970s! A far closer match is the German and Continental 9.3 x 74 rimmed.

Unless you are a professional bear guide in Alaska or spend your summers culling Cape buffalo in Zimbabwe, you are unlikely to "need" one of the real heavies — the calibers of .4 and over. These calibers do recoil, and leave big holes. On the other hand, if you intend to shoot something that "runs both ways," you owe it to both the game and self-preservation to learn to use one. As Robert Ruark wrote back in the fifties "...on anything that can kick me, bite me, claw me, or trample me, I use a Westley Richards .470 double barreled express rifle. I notice that most pros use too much gun, and what's good enough for pros is good enough for me." He would get little argument from his modern counterparts like Ross Seyfried, who did cull Buffalo, or my friend Jim Weaver, a biologist who summered in Zimbabwe and shot — well, a Westley Richards .470 double.

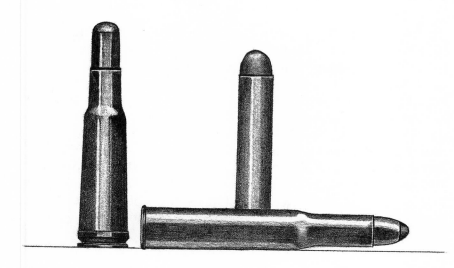

Such calibers are available in short, heavy, but well-balanced, classic double guns by English makers. They resemble the shotguns whose actions they share. Prices on new sidelocks are astronomical, say, three times the cost of my house. Plain sidelocks from between the wars can be had for surprisingly reasonable costs, especially if you are willing to handload a less-than-popular caliber. Brass is available from a number of sources — check *Gun Digest*. Popular "old" calibers include the .416 Rigby — originally a "proprietary" cartridge made by the maker — and .470.

Many modern hunters of real big game prefer bolt-actions. It is certainly possible to get a cheaper (and possible more reliable) gun for the same cartridge in a good bolt-action. I'd stick with claw-type extractors here (discussed in the bolt-action section later.) Alaskan guides will now match a big caliber bolt-action with a plastic stock and a weatherproof finish to make a rainproof bear gun. This is the one case where I would accept plastic. Modern "short" .4s also have a place; they are not designed to reduce recoil (they'll still pound you!) but to work in shorter actions. Examples are the .416 Taylor and .416 Remington. The old cartridges are sometimes *amazingly* long, as well as stout; the .416 Rigby looks like a Minuteman missle.

I should emphasize that the big calibers are a real necessity in certain situations. Father Anderson Bakewell, S.J., explorer, scientist, big game hunter (he took his last cougar, a record animal, at 74 on a horseback hunt, with a recurve bow), and my guru, went after a sloth bear in the Himalayas in the 1940s after it attacked several of his parishoners. He shot it, fatally, with a .30/06. After he got out of the hospital, with scars still visible today, an English officer friend presented him with a "real" rifle, an English bolt-action that he had picked up for $75. Father Bakewell took that rifle to Alaska and the Northwest Territories, shot several bears with it, and still shoots it today. On its bridge is engraved ".416 Rigby Rifle for Heavy Game." I suspect that its now worth 75 *hundred* dollars. He'll never sell it.

And, incidentally: There is no better elk rifle for thick timber and close ranges than a traditional heavy caliber.

Rifles — other than shotgun-style break actions — can be divided into lever- and bolt-actions and single-shots. (Pump and autoloading rifles are even more of an unnecessary evil than pump and autoloading shotguns.)

The lever-action rifle is an American invention, descended from the patents of the ubiquitous John Moses Browning. It was first popularized by Winchester in an amazing array of late 19th century models. All have the familiar "cowboy gun" look; old John Wayne must have killed millions of Indians and rustlers with them in four decades of movies. Winchester lever-actions have slab sides, exposed hammers, a lever beneath the action that encircles your hand, and a magazine tube beneath the barrel.

There are probably more such rifles around than any other kind, which does not mean that they are the best choice for the serious hunter. I am extremely ambivalent about these lever-actions; they are often good but rarely great, and better choices are available.

Their drawbacks are, first, that they are not as accurate as other actions (this may be irrelevant at practical ranges); second, that they are unable to handle "modern" pointed bullets. A pointed cartridge lined up behind another in a lever gun's tubular magazine could strike the primer of the forward cartridge during recoil, causing it to fire the cartridge ahead of *it* in a chain reaction that would destroy the rifle and the shooter's forward hand.* Third, they are not as strong in the action as bolt or single-shot rifles, again making it impossible to use powerful modern cartridges.

If you are a real fan of this most American of all designs, these are not sufficient reasons to avoid the lever-action. You have available a century of usable designs, good guns by both Winchester and Marlin, as well as many Browning limited runs, and a lot of fine old calibers like the .30/30 and .45/70. Their range limitations will simply make you a better hunter. Personally, I'd steer clear of original Model 86s (for the expense and strength; the Browning remakes are reasonable in both regards), post-'64 Winchesters (earlier models are better quality), and new calibers like the .356 and .307 designed to compete with the bolt rifle; if you want a bolt, get one. The classic lever's virtues are in its compact size, its slab sides (which make it a great saddle rifle), its romantic associations, and its traditional mild loads. Don't try to make it into something else.

One special model you might grab if you are an elk or timber hunter is the Model 71 Winchester. The last great lever big bore, it was discontinued in 1957. Made only in the .348 Winchester caliber, these rifles are beautiful, finely detailed, and rugged. Be prepared to pay at least $700 for an original; again, Browning has issued a new version.

But for my mind, there's a better alternative for the lever-action fan than the "cowboy gun" models: the Savage Model 99 I mentioned earlier. Introduced in 1899 and still trim, strong, mechanically ingenious, and "modern," it is the best lever-action ever built. Proof of its effectiveness is that it has been able to digest such nouveau, high-pressure, pointed-bullet cartridges as the .243 and .308; in fact, because of the popularity of these two rounds, it is no longer made in anything *but* .243 and .308.

*The model 1895 Winchester, recently revived by Browning, got around this phenomenon by using a removable vertical magazine that stuck out of the bottom of the action. This protrusion made the gun resemble, in Elmer Keith's vivid phrase, " a poisoned pup that had lain too long in the sun." It was chambered for powerful rounds including the .30/06 and .405 Winchester, was a favorite of Teddy Roosevelt, and is remarkably ugly.

I wouldn't get a new Savage; apart from my lack of enthusiasm about such cartridges (which, really, are perfectly effective), the new Savages are lumpy creations with Monte Carlo stocks and detachable magazines. The "pure" Savage, the one that has survived through the years, been discontinued, and revived again, would be a trim, straight-gripped rifle with a "schnabel" forend in one of Savage's own calibers. It would be chambered for either the wonderful .250 or the factory-designed Savage .300, a useful if slightly redundant round. Such rifles look good. They are compact enough to carry beautifully and point well with the iron sights (or, ideally, peep sights), adequate for ranges under 200 yards.

But the real advantage of the 99 is mechanical. The heart of the classic Savage is a rotating magazine, rather like a revolver's but buried inside the action. (One friend calls the action "a bolt gun with lever attached.") By abandoning the tubular magazine of the other levers, Savage was "ready" for any modern load short enough to fit inside the rather small action body. The Savage action also locks up tighter than the others, promoting greater accuracy. And the motion of the rotating magazine is as slick as grease, with none of the clanking of the Winchester type.

Savage 99s may be the next casualty of our plastic age. Their machining, even on the modern models, is said to be "too expensive." Get one soon, before the collectors begin to hoard them and trade them like "pre-'64" Model 70 Winchesters. Right now you can still get one in .250 and know that you have the early sheep hunter's favorite arm — the gun of Roy Chapman Andrew's Mongolian expedition, a gun used on *tigers* in Asia, not to mention the best rifle for American deer ever invented — all for less than $400. If you want to sacrifice a little theoretical accuracy, you can get one that takes down like a shotgun; some even have auxiliary .410 barrels.

Bolt-actions are the strongest and most accurate form of rifle. Originally late 19th-century military arms, they were soon adopted by sportsmen because of their incomparable long-distance accuracy. They were also able to contain high pressures better than any previously invented action without resorting to the massive and ponderous reinforcements of the shotgun-style double. And the camming action of the bolt could both ram home and extract oversized, misshapen, or pressure-damaged cases that other rifles would not accept.

The first quality bolt rifles were probably built on Continental Mauser actions (the 1898 sporting Mauser, the 1909 Argentine military model) by the bespoke British houses. Americans invented the first great commercial bolt gun to be entirely built by one firm, the Winchester Model 70 (many Mauser actions and stocks were built separately). Simultaneously, there arose an enormous number of custom makers who built rifles on existing Mauser, M70, and military Springfield actions, the best of which make the finest bolt-action rifles — perhaps the finest rifles, period — in the world.

If you want a world-class bolt-action, your best bet is to get a Mauser or Model 70 and take it to such a maker, as I'll discuss a little later. Not all will charge you the price of a Cadillac. The old-style actions are the best for several reasons, the most important being in the design of the bolt itself. In Mausers and old Model 70s, the cartridge is controlled throughout its travel from the maga-zine, to the chamber, to ejection after firing, by a long claw-like extractor attached to the bolt. It is just about impossible to jam such an action — one reason why guides who pursue dangerous game refuse to use other, more "modern," types.

In later years — after 1964 in the case of the Winchester — the positive-acting but expensive-to-make claw was abandoned in favor of a simpler type combined with a recessed bolt head. The recessed head version is alleged to be safer in the rare case of a ruptured cartridge (though one Elwood Epps, writing in the 1977 *Gun Digest*, demonstrated that the "improved" bolt was no guaran-tee against a blown-up rifle) and is certainly cheaper to make. It probably even makes the bolt travel more smoothly. But it does a terrible job of controlling the cartridge; in the words of Albuquerque's master gunsmith Jim Bedeaux, "It just sort of fum-bles it around." Therefore, most knowledgeable gun freaks prefer Mausers and "pre-'64s."

The pre-'64 Winchesters have the added advantage of being highly aesthetic arms, machined from fine steel with hand checkering and precise inletting. They were available in every caliber imaginable, from the pip-squeak Hornet to the elephant-stop-ping .458. The actual '64 Winchesters are atrocities; in addition to the inferior action, they featured pressed checkering, white line spacers, and a barrel channel big enough for a 12-bore shotgun. You could practically stick a book of matches between the stock and the barrel. Winchester and its successor, USRAC, have steadily improved the looks of the M70 in the subsequent years, though keeping to the post-'64 action. Winchester's custom shop will now build you a gun with the older-type action. But it still can be more economical to look for a pre-'64 with a little too much bluing wear on it for the fickle collector. (Pristine specimens tend to cost a *lot.*)

Mausers are always being built somewhere. FN, producer of Browning A5s and Superposeds, makes a fine Mauser action, as does Zastava of Czechoslovakia. Cheap military versions are available everywhere, some excellent, some dangerously worn or fragile. Ask a good gunsmith if you have any doubts. If you want to buy a whole rifle, as opposed to a commercial or military action, your best bet is probably a British Parker-Hale Mauser. This is a beautiful gun, especially in the "Classic" oil-finished, straight-combed model; it is a true Mauser and amazingly inexpensive.

All the quality .22s available today are built on bolt-actions. The collector's pet among them is the discontinued (because of expense) Winchester Model 52. It is extremely accurate, rugged, and well-built, with a great trigger; also, it's extremely expensive, and unless restocked, rather ugly. Browning (of course) makes a new version.

The German firm of Anschutz has built a number of fine rifles in .22, .22 magnum, and .22 Hornet. The Anschutz target actions may be the world's most famous, and the field models are the same internally. Anschutzes tend to Germanic styling, with pronounced pistol grips, schnabel forends, cheek-pieces, and Monte Carlo or curved-top *schweinrucken** stocks. Savage imported them for a while. Anschutzes, like Model 52s, tend to be expensive and very, very accurate. The most accurate unscoped rifle I ever owned was an Anschutz .22 magnum. It had folding leaf sights like an express rifle for African game, and shot better than I could. I sold it

*"Hog back"; similar to the English Greener "rational" stock, if you want to get scholarly.

when I grew dissatisfied with its betwixt-and-between caliber, too light for turkeys, too powerful for squirrels. If it had been a .22 or a .22 Hornet, I would still own it.

The "best buy" in .22s is the Ruger 77/22, a classic-stocked bolt-action that resembles Ruger's big game bolt gun but incorporates the rotating magazine first used in his .22 automatic. It is a superb rifle for about $400.

But the best bolt-action .22 was probably America's highest quality production bolt rifle (or, conceivably, production rifle, period): the Kimber. This rather expensive firearm established a new standard of beauty for the mass-produced gun. The lowest priced Kimber had impeccable styling, good wood, better checkering, and a checkered steel buttplate. Going up in price, you could have added innovative scope mounts, a crisp-edged cheek-piece, an ebony forend tip, and even better wood. A left-handed bolt was available, not a common option in any gun. It is hard to write about the Kimber without using superlatives. Unfortunately, they recently ceased production.

A s I mentioned early in this book; I love single-shot rifles. Part of this affection is aesthetic — no other rifle is as pretty as a falling-block single-shot, a Farquharson or a Ruger. It is the only rifle as beautiful as a fine shotgun. Part is doubtless my romantic notion that, ideally, you should only need one shot on game, and that you should have both the skill to make it count and the restraint not to take it unless you are sure that you can.

And part of it is good sense, if I say so myself. The falling-block action* is strong, nearly as accurate as a bolt, and makes up into a much shorter and quicker-pointing, as well as more beautiful, rifle. It does so without shortening the barrel length — its design eliminates the entire length of the bolt. Or, to put it anothway: A falling-block rifle's stock begins where the *front* of the bolt is located on a bolt-action.

*A falling-block design consists of a massive breech that drops vertically so that the shooter can load the cartridge directly into the chamber, then rises to lock behind it. You work it with a lever under the trigger guard.

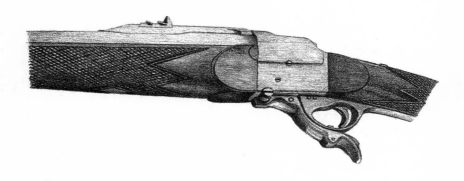

A good falling-block single-shot is also an extremely simple, reliable, trouble-free rifle. Writing in 1948, African guide and former professional ivory poacher John Taylor advised use of a falling block, presumably a turn-of-the-century English design, in preference to a bolt if the aspiring African hunter could not afford a massive double. And he was talking about dangerous game.

Antique American single shots tend to be expensive and, with the exception of some Winchester "high walls," a bit fragile with high-pressure cartridges.* All are romantic, but none as pretty as the British Farquharson and its relatives. Still considered by some to be the best of all falling blocks, the Farquharson is certainly the best looking, though it may not make quite as strong a rifle as the less well known Fraser. Both of these rifles are expensive. I do not know much about the Fraser, but some Farquharsons used to have difficulty extracting tight-fitting cases. There is a better and much less expensive alternative for a working hunter: the Ruger Number 1.

When Bill Ruger came up with the idea for an "obsolete" falling-block rifle in 1966, most sensible people in the firearms business thought that he had lost his mind. But, as usual, his bold

---

* "Low-walls," the lighter actions, can be built into wonderful single-shot .22s by good custom makers.

innovation paid off and triggered a response among those gun nuts not yet numbed to brain death by plastic, Monte Carlos, and pressed checkering. The Number 1 — according to the late Roger Barlow, a perceptive writer who was an early enthusiast, Ruger considered calling it "The Victorian" — resembles a Farquharson, though even cleaner in line. Inside it was all new, much stronger than any English antique (there is no cartridge it will not handle) and capable of ejecting anything. Ruger's "Reactionary Rifle," to borrow another Barlow phrase, is made of chrome-moly steel, stocked in handsome, often figured walnut, and can be ordered in calibers from .22/250 to .458. And it still costs less than $700.

I cannot praise the Number 1 enough. Its graceful yet massive receiver has flat polished sides that draw engravers like flies to honey. The standard model features a slim forend that resembles that of the 19th century Scottish Alexander Henry. The whole gun is short and handy, even in the monster calibers, yet heavy and straight-stocked enough to absorb recoil. It is probably the handsomest action ever designed in the United States, the crown jewel of America's innovative firearms line. It is one contemporary gun that, if there are still gun nuts in the 22nd century, will be collected and, probably, shot.

At the moment, I do not have a Ruger Number 1. I don't have a .375 either. Care to guess what action I will buy when I try again to get a rifle in that caliber?

Custom rifles deserve some attention here. If your experience is anything like mine, you probably encountered the idea of the custom rifle long before you knew exactly what one was. Maybe you saw a bolt-action at the local gunshop that stood out from all the other rifles by virtue of either a slight difference in line or a serious one in wood figure and finish. Maybe you perused the two-page section in the annual *Gun Digest* in which an array of the year's fine rifles, the state of the art in custom guns, is displayed. Or perhaps you saw an article on a gunmaker in a magazine, with sumptuous color photographs that made you say: "I want one of those."

It comes to all of us; it's a human instinct to admire something fine. But in custom guns, you are buying more than craft. You are at least attempting to acquire a tool, something to make you a better hunter. First, for practical reasons, because a custom rifle will fit with your body and your eye and your intellect far better than something made for the nonexistent "average" sportsman. And second, because, well, why shoot a beautiful animal with an ugly gun?

My gun troubles have always run more to buying, trading, coveting, and, sadly, having to sell too many guns. Yet somehow I always thought that having a custom rifle built was only for the rich. I did manage to own a couple of secondhand custom guns (including a 7x57 on a Springfield action) that were very nice — but I never dreamed of having one built for myself. Such things were for millionaires, famous hunters of the past, maybe best-selling novelists or screenwriters, not for struggling freelancers. Besides, I had a subconscious feeling that I didn't know enough.

When the gunmaker asked what barrel or which kind of walnut or even whether I wanted iron sights, would my answer or lack thereof make him look at me in well-disguised contempt or even, you know, laugh at me?

I got through all this the easy way. One day several years ago, I had to have a small repair done on a fine old Belgian double gun, one I didn't want to entrust to anybody unfamiliar with such delicate work. My dealer sent me to Jim Bedeaux of Albuquerque, and I embarked on both a friendship and an education. Jim, now semi-retired, and his son, Roy, are master gunsmiths whose business card reads "Bedeaux: L'Arquebusier" (an archaic French term meaning a builder or user of long guns). They are stockmakers and artists, as well as scholars, amateur historians of the Marine Corps, taletellers, naturalists, and good hosts. Hanging around their shop, talking, watching, and asking questions, I filled in my blanks. I picked their brains as I worked on the first edition of *Good Guns*, and lost my shyness even as I began to see that it hadn't mattered. I realized that you didn't have to be rich to want or afford a custom gun, and decided that "soon" I would have one built.

Late that year, I had to leave New Mexico temporarily. But before I left, I delivered my old Model 70 to Roy. By then we knew each other's tastes and skills so well that I didn't have to specify anything. I had no money, but I was going to be gone for a year anyway. My thought was that Roy would begin a rifle and follow his own ideas to make the ideal old-fashioned sporter, with whatever up-to-date refinements he desired. I joke that my only instructions other than caliber and "good wood" were those of Diaghilev to Stravinsky when he first commissioned a piece of music from the composer: "Étonnez-moi!" (Astonish me!)

The gun is nearing completion now. And not long ago, as we sat around talking about — I hate to admit it — the next project, I thought about my difficulties and misconceptions on the way to my rifle. I returned in a week with a pad of paper, and through a long day of conversation, sometimes supplemented by suggestions from an endless stream of regular customers checking on their projects, we attempted to define and answer the question: How do you go about building a custom rifle?

"What about it, Roy? Why custom?"

"Because it's unique. It's *yours*. I think that if you're interested in something, there's an impulse to get something that fits you, that reflects your tastes rather than anybody else's.

"If getting a custom gun is important to you, you should try it once, even if you never do it again. Some do it only once or twice in a lifetime. Others do it twice a year."

I had decided that my first rifle was to be a 7x57, my favorite caliber, one that would be useful everywhere for my entire life. Still, I am a longtime gun nut with definite prejudices. Where on earth would a beginner start?

"Settle for the basics firsts," Roy advised. "There are three: What cartridge? What type, or which action? And finally, details — your physical build, your taste.

"First, the cartridge. What do you want to accomplish with the gun? No cartridge can do it all. I know some people say the .30/06 can, but I wouldn't use one on brown bears or prairie dogs! You'd better compromise or else plan to own more than one gun."

Two other writers have or are having custom rifles built by the Bedeaux. I took Tom McIntyre to their shop one day a few years ago. In a glass case in their display room was a gun I thought he'd like: a .375 H&H magnum, a long-barreled, heavy, folding-leaf-sighted safari rifle. The stock was made from what appeared to be dark walnut veined in an unusual pattern of fine dark lines, but was actually bubinga, an African hardwood that is extremely dense — and therefore ideal for hard-recoiling express calibers like the .375.

Tom all but drooled. Before he left, he had commissioned a dream rifle for his kind of round-the-world big-game hunting, to be similar to the .375 but in the flatter-shooting .340 Weatherby caliber, suitable for everything from sheep to grizzly. His was to be stocked in walnut, and he sensibly decided that he didn't need the old-fashioned express sights.

On the other hand, I wanted something reasonably light to carry on familiar Western ground, something accurate, something that, with the heaviest handloaded bullets, might be suitable for black bear or even forest elk and that, with light bullets, would be perfect for antelope. A rifle with a little history on it. One good gun. What could be more perfect than the little 7-by, around since the Boer War, Karamojo Bell's ridiculous elephant caliber — small, elegant, low-recoiling.

"One more thing about cartridges before we get too bogged down," said Roy. "The customer should be aware that there are fads in calibers...not that these calibers might not be pretty good, but you'll see a lot of a given caliber for a while, then it'll fade. Right now, all seven millimeters are hot. The .280 Remington is particularly — like it's just been discovered."

(I might point out that at the moment Roy is building four African-express rifles — "elephant rifles" — in .40-plus calibers: a .416 Rigby, a .470, a .404 Jeffery, and a .416 Taylor. Remember, the current popularity of the heavies owes more than a little to sentiment and nostalgia — not a bad thing, but you should be aware of this.)

"Next, actions. There are really only two that have everything — I'm assuming most of your readers will want a bolt-action — and those are the Mauser and the pre-'64 Model 70 Winchester."

"Which is better, Roy?"

"You picked a Model 70...."

"I had one. C'mon, go out on a limb. This is basic, remember?"

"It's hard to say. The best commercial Mausers are the best, period; some of the military ones aren't so good. Model 70s are an improved commercial Mauser for American tastes. You don't have to alter the bolt handle on them. On the other hand, they tend to cost more than Mausers."

"How about saying, 'Some Mausers are better than Model 70s, but 70s are more consistent'?"

"That'll do."

"What about Springfields?"

"Some fine rifles have been built on Springfield actions, but they're even more military than military Mausers — that is, they need more work."

"Model 70? For a beginner?"

"If he doesn't have strong ideas about something else, Model 70."

Next we proceeded to the real hard-core stuff: taste, details, the things that really make a custom rifle someone's "mascot," as engraver Malcolm Appleby might say. Where do we start, Roy?

"First, a person should go to a gunsmith who builds the kind of rifle he likes. We build classic-style rifles here — usually no Monte Carlos, slanting forend tips, or white spacers. If someone asked me to build a thumbhole-stock sporter, I could do it, but I'd be gritting my teeth. He should go to somebody who specializess in such rifles.

"Second, components. I use only Douglas premium-grade barrels. I prefer any button-rifled barrel to one with cut rifling." (In button rifling, a metal button with grooves and lands on its outside is pushed through the barrel, swaging rather than cutting the rifling.)

"Any good, adjustable trigger will do. I'd say that any custom rifle worthy of the name has lapped bolt lugs. The builder should use good, all-steel scope mounts. In general, I'd steer away from alloy parts unless I were building an ultra-light mountain rifle. The goal is to demand acceptable accuracy.

"But don't ask for the lightest *and* the most accurate rifle in the world. Reality puts restrictions on the gunsmith.

"And if you ever do get a six-pound rifle that shoots a three-eighths-inch group, don't sell it. You'll never find another one."

"What about iron sights? I like them, for stylistic reasons, but do you need them?"

"Right. They are not necessary. If you're worried about breaking your scope, take along another scope.

"Scopes are quicker than iron sights. You only have to line up two things: the target and the reticle. And they're more accurate. Besides, I take a lot of time turning down a barrel. I don't particularly like going back and hanging something on the end."

"But there is my seven-by, and there are all those express rifles. *They* all have iron sights...."

"Stylistic consistency is important, too. Your rifle is what you might call a light European sporter. The big ones are English-style heavy game rifles. Both styles demand iron sights."

What you really notice first in a custom rifle is the wood — its color, its grain, its finish. The beauty of a custom rifle is in large part the organic beauty of fine wood, which can be enhanced by skillful work. So at last, we come to the stock. The Bedeaux are riflemakers, "Arquebusiers," who do metal *and* woodwork, unlike many other specialists. But like all fine-gun craftsmen, they have a special place in their hearts for the unique and perfect stocks, no two alike, hidden in the rough-cut blanks.

First, any pointers on stocks?

"We should say something about dimensions here. Your dimensions are a limiting feature. I have a customer who is six-feet, four-inches tall. His stocks are going to look different.

"Wood. French walnut is everybody's favorite. I include Circassian, English, New Zealand walnut in French...and Bastogne, a hybrid, is close. It's dense and easy to work with. It takes fine checkering. It's got the right color.

"I like the reds in Claro. In most cases, it's not as good for checkering. But this is only a general rule. Growing conditions are the important factor in walnut quality. If they are difficult, the conditions are hard, then you're going to get good wood."

Roy diverges from the "classic" orthodoxy on one point. He likes some non-walnut woods as well.

"If you want a non-walnut stock, go for it! I personally like maple. Cherry is beautiful."

Cherry? I had never seen anything but a plain piece of any kind of fruitwood. He pulled down a piece with a feather figure in the butt as impressive as any walnut blank. "Of course, that's rare.

But I'll build in anything the customer wants, so long as it's dense enough.

"Most people realize that you should have a straight grain in the grip for big bores. But really, you can have too much figure. The most beautiful stock blanks I ever say were Turkish Circassian. And they were useless. They would have broken in half the first time they were jarred.

"Also, wood is very subjective. It looks different in a blank. Customers see these exhibition pieces and say, 'I want that.' Exhibition pieces are rare — say, one in three hundred. And they're going to cost, even if you can find one."

We should say something about plastic. "Sure, plastic is certainly a valid material for a custom hunting rifle. More important than plastic's ability to save weight is its imperviousness to moisture."

Any other facts we've missed?

"Details. Not that we can really tell the customer what details he wants. Things like quarter ribs, grip caps, forend tips — the things that make a custom rifle a custom rifle. Those are between the builder and the customer."

Shadows were lengthening. Another visitor brought in beer, and the conversation soon elevated — or fell — to philosophy, to the crotchets of customers and gunsmiths, to disagreements. Roy added that, to forestall future trouble, as much as possible should be worked out beforehand.

"Don't expect a bid. But get an estimate. Commit all your estimates, and even subjective stuff like styles, to paper."

And then, on the second beer, we got around to the two great sources of disagreement: money and time.

"Do we want to talk prices?" I asked. The other customer and I grinned at Roy, who gave us a pleading look.

"You guys know it's almost impossible to get exact prices for work this individual. I'll give you Brownell's price list. But for a unique gun, you'll have to work it out with a gunsmith."

But even money takes second place to time as a potential source of discord between customer and gunsmith. It there is one truism to custom gunmaking, it is that the work takes forever.

According to Roy, "Nowadays people tend to think that if you pay a lot, you should get what you want right away. But it takes time to make something unique. Allow the gunsmith to take that time. Sure, the labor cost is the biggest part of a custom gun.

"But let's say a guy comes in today and says, 'I'll give you $5000 to finish my rifle by the first of July.' Sure, he'll go to the head of the line. He'll get his gun close to on time. It'll shoot well.

"But do you really think it'll be quite as nice as the one built for the guy who says, 'Take your time, get innovative, build me something you'd like to own. I don't care how long it takes'?"

I want to add one thing. It's six years later. Roy has been working on my rifle in his spare time. It is a thing of amazing beauty. It's *almost* done....

8

Hunting Handguns

In the first edition of *Good Guns*, I was at best indifferent to handguns. To quote myself "...handguns for hunting are too new a phenomenon to have much history or lore, and I suspect that they are faddish for most situations."

I'd like to, if not exactly eat my words, modify them. At the time I wrote them, I was still as "Eastern" as I was New Mexican. I was not anti-handgun; in fact, I owned both a single-action .22 revolver and a double-action .357 (definitions in a moment.) But I thought of them as mostly for shooting targets (the .22) and self-defense; I hadn't yet discovered the trail gun.

Another factor was at work, too, one I find less ignorant and culturally biased: I couldn't see the appeal of revolvers with scopes, never mind short single-shot "rifles" with scopes that shot pseudo-rifle calibers. The great virtue of handguns has always been portability; when you load one down with so many accessories that it is awkward to carry, it seems to lose a good part of its *raison d'etre*. And it's still a good deal less accurate (and in almost all cases, less powerful) than even a lever-action .30/30.

Two factors led to my "conversion." One was meeting many Western guides and cowboys who carried either accurate .22s (with which they'd head-shoot such delicious birds as the tame back-country blue grouse) or large-bore revolvers, these most common in the holsters of those who guided hunts for elk, bear, and lions.

The second factor has been the articles of Ross Seyfried, a rancher and magazine writer who is the most worthy heir to Keith and O'Connor and possesses some advantages unknown to either of his predecessors. Mr. Seyfried has taste, experience, and scientific knowledge, as well as (apparently) the money to pursue his obsessions. He is the only "gun writer" in the U.S. to produce a steady flow of information on African calibers, Damascus shotguns, English "Bests," and custom big-bore handguns. He kills Cape buffalo with them, not as an isolated stunt, but as a natural culmination of years of study and buffalo culling. He loves wild animals, old guns, and good writing. He even has a sense of humor.

In Seyfried's writing on handguns, I discovered the mind of a kindred spirit, one whose knowledge was far in advance of my own. His thesis is that a "handgun" is a portable weapon with iron sights, and that if you are not ready to learn the art of shooting within its inherent limitations, you should use a rifle or stay home.

He is also a "Keithian." In handguns, large caliber is even more important than in rifles, for it is impossible to build up the velocity of a handgun load to the power of a rifle without making it impossible to shoot. (The short barrels also influence velocity.) *Big holes kill cleanly.*

With his example, and that of my local friends, I have begun to appreciate the "country handgun." Its portability — your hands are always free — and the challenge of learning to use one properly have become a fascination. What follows is a little information and a few prejudices. I shall continue to learn, and report.

Most backcountry handguns are either revolvers or .22 autopistols. Large-bore autopistols are not generally powerful enough or accurate enough for killing game reliably.

Revolvers are divided into two types. "Single-action" revolvers are the cowboy-style guns with the smoothly curved handles familiar to anyone who grew up seeing Westerns. You must cock the hammer to fire a single-action revolver; pulling the trigger without cocking it does nothing. The cylinder of a single-action gun does not swivel out, though it can be removed. You load it from a "gate" on the right side. (This slightly awkward placement makes some historians think that Mr. Colt was left-handed.)

"Double-action" revolvers are the police type, as opposed to the cowboy type. Typically, they have an angled "break" between the grip and the rest of the action. Their cylinders swing out (to the left) to reload. You can fire them by a steady (hard) pull on the trigger, or by cocking them like a single-action, hence, "double."

A few principles apply to all revolvers — and to all handguns. Bigger, heavier, and above all longer-barreled all make for greater steadiness and less recoil. (Until they become a problem in themselves. Perhaps my own modest size and small hands are a contributing factor, but I find the Ruger double-action .44s too big to handle comfortably.)

And: few "factory" handguns grips are satisfactory. You have smaller fingers on the "bottom" of your hand; why are grips bigger there? Most double-action grips are too big all over. Single-action grips tend to be better. The Ruger "Bisley" and the mighty Casull grips are the best of all.

Specifics. There are three general types of good single-actions available: Colts and their clones; Rugers; and the Casull. The Colt single-action "Army" is the prototypical cowboy single-action. Like the fine double shotgun, it is basically a 19th- century design. Like the double, it is elegant and light and simple. Like the double, you pay something extra for it, especially if you have Colt build you one today.

It has limitations. You cannot load it up with monstrously hot loads the way you can a Ruger without blowing your hand off. This is not as much a limitation as it might be; old "long Colt" .45 loads are pretty powerful at close ranges. But the sights are also fixed and pretty rudimentary. Colts are not really hunting weapons, though they are okay as backup guns.

Several European companies, especially Uberti of Italy, make replicas that my friends and I refer to as "Spaghetti Colts." The is *not* a term of contempt. They are available in more models for less money and time than any product of the Colt shop. They are said to be made of stronger steels. The best of them are so well-machined that their parts interchange with Colts. You will not have the romance, but you will have the best buy.

Ruger single-action revolvers are available in all calibers from .22 to .44 magnum and .45 Colt. They are a bit bulkier than Colts, feature investment-cast parts, and (except in the new Vaquero model, which superficially resembles a Colt) have adjustable sights. In .44 and .45, they can be loaded to pressures that would vaporize a Colt. Master gunsmith John Linebaugh of Wyoming builds incredible customer revolvers in huge "propri-etary" calibers on Ruger actions; Seyfried has killed buffalo with his. On the other end of the spectrum, you can get a lightweight revolver with interchangeable .22 and .22 magnum cylinders. Rugers are made in stainless steel as well as blued steel, if you want a low-maintenance tool.

My first choice in a Ruger would be a mildly custom rig built on the "Bisley" action, which has a more hand-filling grip, a lower hammer, and a steel frame on the .22. (Other Ruger .22's have an alloy frame.)

And all Rugers are ridiculously cheap as well as strong. Their triggers should (and can easily) be improved.

The Casull revolvers from Freedom Arms are not cheap, nor do they need improvement. They're deceptively simple five-shot, single-action revolvers of softly burnished stainless steel, made to tolerances that would not shame Purdey's. You can get one in caliber .454 Casull that would probably stop a close-in grizzly. At well under $2000, they are a relatively cheap door to perfection. They also make a .22; it's still a five-shot gun, and remarkably heavy.

While I admire all of the above-mentioned single-actions, I become far more partisan about double-actions. In two words: Smith & Wesson. Colt fans may howl, but I (and others) have found their double-action guns to be less reliable, prone to breakage, less comfortable in the hand, less well-designed. They *are* well-finished on the outside, but even in this respect I find their high-end guns edging into *too* brightly finished. Ruger double-actions are strong, but clunky and unaesthetic to my eyes.

Although handgun hunters in the past have steered toward single-actions (you don't usually shoot at a game animal with a heavy double-action pull), Smith's double-actions come out of the box with a trigger pull in the single-action "mode" that is as fine as anything I've ever bought, shaming Ruger's. Smith & Wesson make so many models that it's hard to single one out; cynics refer to their "gun of the month." Smith hunter-styled "Classic" .44s may be the best out-of-the-box hunting handguns available after Casulls, that cost three times as much. They even have good grips! And, although their old .44s had a reputation for being more fragile than Ruger's, the new ones have been re-designed to shoot heavy loads for a lifetime. They are the handsomest and most aesthetic double-actions around. I own two.

My bargain choice for a double-action gun would be the newer models of Brazil's Taurus. Their quality control is excellent. Though it may be heresy, I like them better than the other American double-actions, especially for the money. They even make a .44 special, a fine but neglected caliber.

Calibers. Basically, there are two: .22s, and "above .44." The .22 handgun is useful for killing rabbits and grouse. Accurate ones are not expensive. Ammunition is positively cheap, so you can practice a lot and become a good shot. Even if you want to shoot big bores, the only way that you are likely to become accurate is to practice *a lot* with a .22. Handgun accuracy is not as easy as rifle accuracy.

I should add that there are several fine autopistols in .22 that are worthwhile back-country guns, some of which achieve match-level accuracy. The Colt "Woodsman" model, no longer made, brings premium prices and is a favorite of mine; I wish I still owned one. The High-Standard was cheaper and could be as accurate; it is being revived. The Ruger, with a target-style bull barrel, is a "best buy"; I wish it were easier to take down for cleaning. The Browning Buck Mark and the (expensive) S&W are other good choices.

The reason I do not advocate so-called big-bore autopistols for the backcountry (although I own a 1911-type .45) is that they aren't really *big*. Even the "mighty" .45 A.C.P. (Automatic Colt Pistol), although its diameter is large enough to make a big hole in an attacker, is a tiny round compared to any rifle load. The much more powerful .44 magnum still looks pretty wimpy beside a factory-loaded .30/30 rifle. Don't believe everything you see in the movies.

If you are going to hunt deer, you should start with a .22 and learn to shoot, then move up to something like a stout (Western for "heavy") .44. But use mild .44 special loads before you go up to full-strength .44 magnums... handgun accuracy is difficult enough to achieve even if you aren't flinching.

All the .38 calibers, including the .357, are inadequate on deer-sized game. *They will not kill reliably*. Period.

Confine yourself to shots well under 100 yards. Elmer Keith shot (and Ross Seyfried shoots) things at greater distances with handguns. When you're that good, you won't need any advice from me.

If you get serious about this demanding method, you'll probably pass the .44. At this point, the Casull and Linebaugh calibers become interesting. Again, you'll probably need no advice.

A nd one last word: snakes. I do not shoot snakes. If you are so afraid of snakes that you think you need shotgun-style "snake-loads" in your handgun, maybe you'd best re-think your reasons for being in the backcountry. I live in one of the snakiest regions of the U.S. (we have six species of rattlers) and have never had to shoot one. I often carry a couple of snake rounds in the summer when I have my dog with me, so I could protect him if I had to. But he is as cautious as I am, and always backs away from the snakes, barking. I have killed one snake in my fourteen years here;   I broke its back while trying to extricate it from my pigeon loft with a snake stick. I have "moved" a dozen others without incident.

This is not sentimentality. I reserve the right to kill a big diamondback if it invades my yard; they're too big and aggressive for me to handle safely. But when you are in the wilderness, does it make any sense at all, in the late 20th century, to eliminate a terrified little predator out of some atavistic primate dread? Save your rounds! Humans, sadly, are far more dangerous than rattlesnakes.

9

Problems

I am probably better qualified to write this chapter than I am for any of the others. I have never counted the dollars that I spent learning how many mistakes can be made by one person; it's probably best for my sanity that I never attempt to do so.

What to pay for a gun? This one I can't tell you. Even if our tastes were the same and all dealers charged standard prices, inflation and the tides of fashion that move even the conservative gun world would invalidate my comments in a year. The various "gun-buyers' guides" can therefore be only of limited use, though perhaps good for comparative values. Your best bet for finding current prices is to check the pages of *The Shotgun News* (available in many large gun stores) or *The Gun List.* The second is much easier to use, as it classes its guns alphabetically and has a table of contents. But even these lists will not help you on oddities like the products of the small English or Belgian shops. This is the point where having a dealer you can trust becomes important, and where the three-day inspection provision becomes useful. Have your gun shipped, check it over in the company of your expert, and then make your decision. Even if you want a particular gun desperately, pay attention to his advice. Apart from the cost of fixing any major fault, anything that is not "as advertised" may well become a disappointment as you gain in knowledge.

So sell it, you say? The "gun as investment" idea may be the biggest scam alive today. Considering the dealer's legitimate markup, you will be unlikely to make a profit on the resale of even a *good* old gun, unless you're a dealer. On a dog, or on a piece like a Parker that carries a lot of "fad" inflation, you will be very lucky to get what you paid for it. One possible exception is a top-of-the-line English Best — you may not make a profit on the sale of a Best, but you will be unlikely to lose money on it if it is sound.

So you've decided you want a real game gun, whether because you've seen how pretty they look in the racks at the sporting dealers, or because you have a friend with taste and experience, or from reading magazines. Maybe you've been shooting something pretty good — say, a straight-stocked, Japanese-made over-under that points well but that isn't quite as pretty as the nameless English boxlocks in the Barbour ads. Maybe you've got a nice old family L.C. Smith that looks beautiful and is worth a lot, with golden walnut and burnished barrels, but in the uplands, you know it handles like a log, your next birthday is your fortieth, and it weighs 7½ pounds....

Anyway, you want something elegant and light, with two barrels arranged the proper way, beside each other like your eyes. You want it to carry easily and look pretty and, well, last forever. You don't have twenty or thirty or even twelve thousand dollars to spend on a gun, but you want one that will please you as much as if you did.

So what do you do? The advertising columns of the quality gun magazines are full of guns — famous names with high prices, many more obscure ones with lower ones. Some friends tell you to get a Spanish gun; others tell you that Spanish guns are junk. You look at the prices and realize that the better Spanish guns now can go for five, even six thousand dollars. Everybody has an opinion. You need a drink.

I can't tell you what to do . I can't tell you what names to buy. Guns, even in top condition, are too individual for me to tell you a price-to-value ratio, even if your tastes are the same as mine. The only way I could be sure to satisfy you would be to advise you to go to a top London maker — Purdey, Holland, Evans, Boss, Wilkes — and get yourself measured. I'd virtually guarantee satisfaction (if not shooting prowess, which can only be achieved, not bought) if you did that. But we've already agreed that you don't have thirty thousand minimum for a gun.

I *can* tell you a few things. The focus of today's lesson will be on quality, and how to discern it. We will go briefly over first principles of a game gun. (I will assume you already have some idea of what a game gun is, or you would not be reading this.) We will discuss the difference between quality and condition, and look even more briefly at condition, which, although necessary if you are to get your money's worth, is not the subject of this lesson. However, we will look at a few defects of condition that will render quality beside the point. We'll touch on proof.

We'll look for indicators of quality. We will discuss 16-gauges, a few American guns, Italy, Spain, and the products of the Belgian guilds. We will name a few names, if only to remind you that names are not what this is all about. We will tell you to first be cautious, then be bold. And finally, we'll even dare to make a stab at the price range we're discussing. All opinions here are mine. I've earned them through two decades of maniacal shooting and trading. They may be wrong, but although they are subject to modification through learning, they will not be changed by shouting at me. I *already know* I'm an idiot. We'll start with the tangibles.

G AME GUNS: Side-by-side shotguns made to shoot moderate loads at upland game birds at moderate distances. They should be light enough to carry all day, yet heavy enough to swing smoothly. Twelves should weigh between 6 and 6¾ pounds, 16s between 5½ and 6. Some people whom I respect want 20s and 28s to weigh much like the 16 on the grounds that otherwise they are too light and whippy. I think they can get a bit lighter as long as they have long barrels. One the other hand, any 28 with all the virtues we are about to specify will cost too much. Can we agree to ignore the .410?

BARRELS: These should be over 26 inches, up to 30. I consider 28 the ideal length, but will live with any in this range; 26-inch barrels are ugly and whippy. All, *regardless of gauge and length*, should weigh under three pounds. A little under for a 12, less for the smaller bores. Long and light. Oh, and...watch out for cut barrels. Anybody who would cut off the barrels on a balanced, hand-finished gun would probably get cosmetic surgery or cut his dog's vocal cords to stifle her bark.

TRIGGERS: They should have two. No less a connoisseur of guns than the novelist Thomas McGuane disagrees on this, and Tom has gone through a couple of Bosses, and shoots more than I do. "Look at the grace of that little trigger guard," he says, pointing to the undeniably elegant curve on his current beautiful sidelock. I agree. But for me, two not only work better, they're mechanically simpler. Besides, look at the great round bow of a trigger guard on turn-of-the-18th century Manton game guns. They're still graceful! I just like two better. Sorry, Tom.

GRIPS: Game guns should have straight-hand grips. I am willing to make some allowance for the French-type semi-pistol— the round knob, but slimmer than that on the old Browning— or the Prince of Wales, the capped English version of same. At least it's relatively easy to cut off.

BALANCE: Nothing is harder to convey in words, or is easier to recognize. It does *not* mean light or barrel-light. Balanced guns swing smoothly. See long and light, above. See also the kind of hand workmanship that adjusts stocks to barrels.

Enough on definition.

Quality and condition and "collectibility" and other cans of rotten worms.

First, you can have an unfired A-grade Parker that is worth $60,000 and still not have what I'll call game gun *shootable* quality. It will be a nice gun. It will be pretty, at least to some eyes. It will be valuable. Its wood will be excellent. And it will probably handle like an I-beam. But, of course, you wouldn't want to shoot a gun like that.

To a collector, mint condition is important. To the English shooter — who, like it or not, has given us our most workable standards of quality for upland guns that feel alive in our hands, that work with us to make us better shooters — any old gun that you acquire is but a template for your perfect gun, not the perfect gun itself. You should not worry too much about extended stocks, shortened stocks (you can modify both), or rubbed bluing. Chokes should be open anyway. More on modification later in this book.

You *should*, however, check proof. If the dealer doesn't know what it means, you should probably go to another dealer (unless he's offering you a clean-looking Purdey for $1000, and in that case it's probably been stolen within the hour). If he's offering Purdeys for $12,000 and still doesn't know what it means, *run* to another dealer.

Do not mess with extended chambers — and I mean, especially in English guns, ones of 2¾ inches — unless the gun has been reproved in England. Nowadays, 2½-inch ammunition is not hard to come by, even if you live in darkest New Mexico as I do.

Measure the barrels. Look for suspicious spaces between the ends, or odd lengths. Do not buy a set of shortened barrels unless you want to pay well up in four figures for a new set. And if you can do that, why are you looking for a buy? We will discuss sleeving later.

Oh, and — *if* you know a lot about them — *good* Damascus guns are fine. I know everybody told you they were as dangerous as rattlesnakes. Everybody doesn't know what he's talking about. I'll come back to this a little later.

Enough on condition.

You are in a real gun shop (or shopping in a good detailed catalog with a return privilege) where the owner knows what proof is. In front of you are a $7000, brand-new Italian 12; a $700, 20-bore, boxlock Spanish gun; a $2000 sidelock Spanish 28; an A.H. Fox, a beautifully engraved 12, for $3000; a boxlock Belgian 12 for $2500; and finally, an English 16, by a maker with a name so obscure you've never even read it, for $3500. You have $3000 in your pocket, and it's going to hurt, because you are a freelance writer whose '79 pickup truck is going to need a valve job yesterday. We will assume you are going home with a gun. You are an addict, or you wouldn't be reading this.

The first gun is very beautiful, and you know Italian guns have a reputation for being strong, for having good steel. It, and the cheapest Spanish gun, are the only new guns in the store. The price is absurd — but maybe the dealer, a friendly acquaintance who likes your articles, will take a few installments.

And God, it's a sidelock. The highly polished lockplates carry fine rose-and-scroll engraving that looks to you like that in the photos of the Purdey in the last catalog full of impossibles you got from Sotheby's.

I'm looking over your shoulder here. Point the barrels at the light and let it run down them. They're smooth, aren't they? No ripples. That's good — they have been draw-filed lengthwise. All handmade doubles are, some, but on this one the surface is perfect.

Aesthetics? It's a little bright for me. The blue is so highly polished that it looks like the barrel of a Weatherby rifle. And that silvery so-called "coin-finish," which you get on most new Spanish and Italian guns these days, is not my favorite. Still, it's well done.

Fling it up to you shoulder. What does it feel like? Not sure? Not a good sign, at least for the very best. Your reaction should be more like, "Oh, my God." Let me...yes, it's...okay. But no cigar. How heavy? Seven pounds? With 26-inch barrels? And a single trigger? Come here a minute. (Whispered: Look, it's beautiful and well-made and will last forever. But it's awfully clunky for $7000. Which you don't have.)

Yeah, sure, let's look at that Spanish gun — the 20. No, it's not as pretty as the others. What do you expect for $700? Bright finish again, right? And there are some tool marks around the corners. And the engraving is obviously machine-made. But don't just throw it back...it has some virtues, too. Look: 28-inch barrels, and I'll bet it's a good bit under six pounds. Nice stock dimensions. (Whispered: It's a lot closer to balanced than the 12 was.) A checkered butt, no frills. Nice.

Oh, right, show off. Yes, the barrels have a bit of ripple on their surfaces — just a mild aesthetic defect, but you're right. And hey — there's a lifetime warranty on repairs for the first owner. You don't get that with any American gun.

Okay, okay, I do shoot something better myself. But I'd rather carry this one all day than the 12. And you could fix your truck. Right. Let's see the other Spanish gun.

Sure is pretty. Hand detachable sidelocks — real "trick," as a Texas friend used to say. Let's take them off. Oooh — gold-plating on the interior parts. The English and Belgians used to do it to resist rust. Think you need it on a gun you use on quail? When was the last time you hunted quail in the rain? 1979? You want to use it on Maine woodcock, too? Let me give you a tip: Don't take the locks off unless you drop it in the river and it stays down more than ten minutes. *Especially* don't pull them off when you just had three Scotches and want to show your friends how cool the gold is. You'll chip the wood on the edges and then water'll really get in. Some London gunshop once told an owner that they didn't make hand-detachable sidelocks because a gentleman never took his guns apart. I won't go that far, but he was making a point.

The bluing is good. None of that mirror-bright nonsense...a soft gray-blue. No ripples. Nice.

Yes, you have the idea. The stock dimensions are fine, high and long. But it waves around like a .22 pistol. Whoever got the bright idea of putting 25-inch barrels on a — what, five-pound — 28-gauge? I know some people who could shoot it. But I couldn't hit the damn ground with it. You could carry it all day. One-handed. You might be able to do pretty well with it on rising woodcock. But as an all-around gun, I'd pass.

Ah, the Fox. As the years pass, I begin to buy Michael McIntosh's idea that it was the best gun ever made in America, overall. Or at least, certain variants can be.

Hmm. Gorgeous wood. The engraving's sort of coarse, but not cartoonish like on some Ithacas; more like a German gun, or a Greener from Birmingham. Handsome, in fact. Fine condition on the wood. Probably restored — see the red Pachmayr pad? — which doesn't bother me a bit.

But, damn, it's even clunkier than the Italian gun. Beavertail, pistol grip — God, if there's ever a reason for a gun with a single trigger, it's on a gun with a curved grip like this — you can't comfortably move your hand from trigger to trigger. And heavy — it's, what, 7½? Not an upland gun for me.

I do like the shape of that Fox action, though. And the indestructible sturdiness. They have too much collector value — price, in simple words — to refinish. Tell you what I'd do if I wanted an American gun and could pay the price: I'd look for a Fox 16 or a 20, with a diamond cross-section, straight-hand grip. In an American gun, you could probably get away with 26 inches and have good balance. They say Aldo Leopold's 20 had a grip like that and weighed 5½ pounds....

Yes, let's see that Belgian gun. No name? Not necessarily a problem. Though maybe the price should be a bit lower.

Hmm... (Whispered: This is the sleeper. It's made like an English gun. Jeez, look at the details. Those oak-leaf fences; and the scroll on the sides is much finer than that imitation Purdey crap on the Spanish and Italian guns. Little gold cocking indicators. The checkering is almost too fine — that's a Continental habit. You can barely feel it. Control yourself. Maybe we can get him to knock the price down.)

The wood looks dark. Age and oil. But I thinks there's some real figure under there. It doesn't take a master craftsman to refinish a stock if you go slowly.

Prince-of-Wales grip. That should bring the price down a little, too. But it works almost like a straight grip. Long barrels. Twenty-seven, nearly. That's a standard Continental length. No problem. Shoulder it and...aah, I can see you just figured something out. It's a big gun, maybe almost as heavy as the Italian or the Fox, but it points like magic. Makes you grin, doesn't it? So much for the O'Connor dictum of short barrels in the uplands.

And here's the one *I've* been looking at. It's English, which does matter, though not as much as snobs think. (Don't forget the Belgian 12.) And it's a 16.

Why does that matter? Because, first, it's conceivably the best combination of light weight and potent shot charge for the uplands. Six-pound gun for a one-ounce load...can't beat it.

But also, people — the English as well as the Americans — just sort of pass it by. The English have always preferred 12s. Sixteens were for women, kids, old buffers, or naturalists in the tropics who actually carried their own guns. (Lucky women, kids, etcetera.) And the Americans have always either wanted to stuff

10-bore duck loads into 12s, or show off with toys like that little 25-inch sidelock. They pay more for both, on both sides of the Atlantic. Which leaves the 16s for smart people like us.

Other nice things about English 16s — they tend to weigh right, look right, and have 28-inch barrels. But let's look at this one.

Yes. All of the above. Don't worry, I'll let you handle it in a minute. Oh, all right...here. Feel that grip, the shape of it. Diamond-shaped in cross-section, as I mentioned when we were looking at the Fox. Helps keep your grip the same, prevents canting — and feels good. As, I can see from your face, does the balance. And it's lighter than the Belgian.

Dark? Well, yes it is. A lot of English guns have their walnut stained rather dark — don't know why, unless it's the usual English dread of being flashy — unlike, say, the Italians. You can always refinish it, but since I have both, plus Irish and German, in my blood, I'm not taking any sides here. I like the dark case colors. It still has a lot, too.

Have I heard of Ballocks of Kent? No. So what? If I had, it might cost $8000 like Westley Richards of Birmingham or more, like Purdey's of London.

It has 2½-inch chambers. No problem, as I said. Order the ammunition by the case, and it's cheaper than buying single boxes of American ammo over the counter.

(A voice from being the counter intervenes.) You have a Damascus English gun in the back room? Bring it out! Oh my God, a hammer Purdey. Look at this — 30-inch Damascus barrels, snap underlever. No pits in the bores. Is it in proof? Oh boy....

You've got to consider this one! The price is the same as the Ballocks. It's black-powder proof, 2½ -inch, so you'd have to handload. It's a little heavy, but the balance is perfect. Extractor gun, the only one here — that just makes it easier to save the old shells..

Oh, right. Excuse me. Just got a little carried away there. One of the best shots in Texas says that God the Father shoots a hammer underlever Purdey. And if you do want a great name like Purdey or Westley for a good price, you'd best look for a Damascus hammer gun.

Well, what do you think? I'd say the best value-to-price ratios are in the cheap Spanish gun, the Belgian, and the Ballocks.

(And by the way, did you notice they are all boxlocks? Some writers contend that only British sidelocks can be properly balanced. That's just plain nonsense. Because of their construction, a boxlock's weight distribution is a little different from that of a sidelock, but any competent handmaker should be able to deal with this "problem." As far as the country of origin, the English do make a greater number of perfectly balanced guns than anybody else, but I've seen excellent Belgians and pretty fair French, Italian, even Spanish guns.)

No, the Spanish isn't as pretty, or as magical in the handling. You could fix your truck. But I'm reminded of the wonderful trout-fishing writer John Gierach, who was asked how someone with a leaky roof and a 20-year-old pickup could afford his collection of vintage cane rods. "Isn't it obvious?" he replied.

The Belgian won't impress your friends like an English gun, but then whoever heard of Ballocks? Still, maybe there's a little better value-to-the-dollar in the 16. You might bring the deal down a little on either if they've been here for a while, but really, both prices are fair.

The hammer Purdey? Be careful. That way lies madness....

Stock alterations, especially in shotguns, are a complicated case. Only a fanatic would object to a high quality, oil-type-finished, re-checkered stock renovation. Go to a *good* gunsmith. Do not insult the gun by having some hack slather on a high-gloss coat of modern poly-whatsis. Such finishes are ugly and crass; they flake and flash like mirrors.

Alterations in dimensions are a more complicated and ambiguous case. In a shotgun, too much drop or a radically too short or long stock, or one that bends in the wrong direction, can cause you to miss. But most stocks, especially those on American guns, are crafted to fit a mythical average shooter and thereby sort of fit everybody.

Even if you decide to have a custom gun or stock made, there are some complications. While both Purdey and others in London and Orvis and others in the U.S. will take your measurements (Purdey sends a representative on a tour of the U.S. every year to do just that and you don't have to commit to a gun), Purdey's stock length will often come out longer. The English believe in long stocks — fifteen inches is a common length there, though in America almost unknown except on trap guns.*

If in doubt, you might go with the longer length; theoretically, the more experience you have, the longer stock you can shoot. (And, I might add, my experience has seemed to indicate the opposite. I am now shooting with a shortened stock on my Simonis.)

Which only goes to show you that the road of stock mysticism is a dangerous one to travel. Go slowly. More on fit in the next chapter.

Rifles are easier. Almost anybody can shoot with almost any rifle stock. Some 99s are made with too much drop for scopes. I had a laced-on leather pad on mine, a lighter solution than the factory Monte Carlo, and less expensive than a custom stock.

Metal refinishing is one area where my opinions and those of the purists coincide — don't. Rubbed, silvered bluing is a badge of honorable wear, faded case-colors an inevitable and harmless sign of age. Ninety-nine percent of the people you will take your gun to for work will buff off the crisp metal edges to prepare it for a reblue that it doesn't need, ruining its resale value, and, more importantly, hurting its looks. Hardly anybody today can do case colors well; those who do advertise and are known. Classic firearms demand a soft rust blue, not the glaring, brilliant high-gloss jobs that most backyard experts will give them. Leave well enough alone until you know what you are doing. Then you'll probably *want* to leave well enough alone.

Now, let's say you have just found the perfect rifle, but it's in some weird caliber. Should you buy it and re-chamber and/or re-barrel? Maybe. First, find out if it's possible; for example, converting many bolt-action rifles to .375 H&H is impractical because of the unusual length of the cartridge. If the gun is an irreplaceable collector's item, it would probably be a dumb idea, though mere cost will probably preclude the idea in such cases.

* American standard is about 14½ inches.

Since Model 70s are now "collectibles," some purists object to a shooter's converting one into a custom gun. If the gun is a super-grade .375 personally used by Ernest Hemingway, they may have a point. If it's a beat-up .30/06 with no bluing that has been carried to elk camp in New Mexico for years, why not fix it up a bit? Of course, its history as is may be just as interesting as the other's.

Black powder guns exist mostly beyond the self-imposed boundaries of this book. But American shooters often seem confused by the subject of Damascus barrels. You've all seen Damascus wallhangers — hammer guns with 32-inch barrels bearing faint spiral traces, aged Parkers and English muzzleloaders marked with intricate, almost three-dimensional rings of whorls, like fingerprints or the coils of fossil shells. Their varying colors, with gray steel etched into faded silver or a mix of warm firelit browns, are as alive as those of old walnut and make the hard blue-black of modern arms look cold. When you pick them up, their grace and liveliness give you an instant kinship with shooters of their time. You know you could shoot one of these....

And instantly the chorus goes up, "You can't! Damascus is deadly." Shooting one means an instant loss of your left hand as the barrel explodes like a bomb. Damascus is for black powder only. Damascus is unsafe even *with* black powder. Damascus is made of old horsehoe nails, was immediately abandoned when fluid steel became available, was a bad idea even when it was in common use — didn't you know that old-time shooters held their forward hand on the forend because of the frequency of burst barrels? Better just hang that Damascus gun on the wall, which is why I'm only asking $100 for it.

Or maybe you could sleeve it with steel barrels. Of course, that'll cost you about the price of a modern shotgun, and the end product might not balance as well as the original. Nor will it be as pretty. But it'll be *safe*.

Meanwhile, Douglas McDougall, English sporting writer and big-bore expert, crouches in a Scottish field, glassing for grey-lag geese. Beside him stands a magnum 8-bore Tolley double gun. It is 100 years old, with an underlever, graceful hammers, and back-action locks. A small party of geese turns and swings by just within range, at perhaps sixty yards. McDougall stands up, swings through, and fires. A goose falls, certainly more than the 1000th goose that has fallen to that great gun. The load that killed it is three full ounces of No. 1 shot, backed by modern smokeless nitro powder, shot through barrels of — what else? — fine Damsacus.

Of course, the monster magnum is an extreme example, but it serves to show the modern shooter that some of his ideas about Damascus may be in need of revision. But first, what *is* Damascus? Well, to start with, it's a misnomer. True Damascus steel was made by a method of forging sword blades developed in Syria more than 1000 years ago in which a cake with layers of iron and steel was heated, flattened, folded, hammered, folded, and so on, making a blade of superior strength and hardness that held an edge as well as some modern stainless steels and actually — because of microscopic serrations between the iron and steel — may have cut better. Strictly speaking, twisted and welded gun barrels of mixed iron and steel should be called Damascus only by analogy.

What about some of the notions mentioned earlier? Horseshoe nails? There's some truth in that accusation, but it hardly says anything bad about Damascus barrel quality. The first spiral barrels in fowling pieces were often called "stub barrels" because they were made from the stubs of old horseshoe nails. As W.W. Greener said in the first edition of his famous *The Gun and Its Development*: "The nails have always been made from the very best iron, and are also considered to obtain some virtue from the contact with the horse's hoof." These barrels did not have the complicated "fingerprints" of later Damascus, because the sandwich bars of iron and steel were simply wrapped around a central mandrel.

Soon, innovative gunmakers found that twisting the bars, and using more separate strands of iron and steel in them, increased both strength and beauty. By the mid-1800s, one maker in Belgium — always the great center for Damascus barrel-making — used as many as 300 separate strips on the bar! Usually they were twisted in about eight turns to the inch, but some ornate Belgian barrels had as many as eighteen twists. After the strips had been rolled and welded, each maker's composition made an identifiable pattern, which might be enhanced by acid etching — this dissolved the upper surface of the iron, leaving the steel standing out in relief — or browning. Bluing was less common, as it hid rather than enhanced the pattern.

And what about safety? The idea that old-time shooters held onto the forend close in toward the action was true in the days of muzzleloaders, but for reasons having little to do with Damascus barrrels. It has always been possible to double-charge a muzzle-loader barrel if the shooter isn't careful, and it is harder to detect that a barrel is blocked by mud or snow when you can't peer down the barrels from the breech. Such situations — or their modern equivalent, such as dropping a 20-gauge shell into the chamber of a 12-gauge gun where it can lodge ahead of a 12-gauge shell — will produce barrel bursts in amost any modern gun. (The M21 Winchester was *proofed* this way.)

But this trouble no longer existed when breechloading cartridge guns became popular — say, after the 1860s. Still, Damascus guns continued to dominate the scene, despite the fact that, according to Greener, "modern"-type fluid-steel barrels had existed in some form since 1808. They had their own problems; flaws in Damascus barrels would show themselves in manufacture and, because of the composite nature of the barrels, were in any case likely to be much smaller.

To be fair to those who are against Damascus, its proponents had some pretty strange ideas, too. Many thought that twist barrels would merely expand slightly if an oversized charge passed through them, when in fact any bulging is a sign of imminent barrel failure. Still, Damascus persisted until the First World War as the material of choice in fine shotgun barrels, and its decline probably owed as much to the expense of its manufacture — fine Damascus costs more than fliud steel — as to its inferiority with smokeless powder. Even so, some Belgian companies made Damascus barrels at least into the 1970s!

Nowadays there are a lot of fine old Damascus guns around. There are also a lot of dubious ones. *I am not advocating your shooting Damascus guns*, not in these days of product liability suits and other such abdications of personal responsibility. No Damascus gun was designed for smokeless powder — never mind magnum loads — and the "fool killer" will surely harvest anyone who thoughtlessly puts modern shells through a vintage weapon. Don't do it!

But do consider the following: First, the English will shoot certain nitro (smokeless) loads through appropriate Damascus guns. "Appropriate" means that the shooter has sent his gun to the government proof house in London or Birmingham, where the proof authorities stress-test it with extra-powerful loads. Guns that pass such tests are "guaranteed" by all the conservative majesty of this remaining outpost of British tradition. I have never heard of one blowing up afterward. Of course, it goes without saying that you don't shoot loads that exceed the amount of powder or shot stamped on the barrel, the maximum load that is guaranteed.

And also, of course, some guns are blown up in proof. If you don't want to risk destroying some gorgeous antique, you can have an English gunsmith check to make sure that the gun has not been bored out to remove pits, thereby dangerously weakening the barrels by thinning them to paperlike dimensions. (I assume that if the gun does have internal pits, you will only use it as a wallhanger.)

And what about American guns? There are more than a few complications here. First, since we have never had a mandatory government proof, our guns do not have the maximum load stamped beneath the barrels to give us an amount of shot and pressure that we cannot exceed. Second, our modern shells are longer than the chambers of any Damascus gun, U.S. or English. Most Damascus guns have chambers of 2½ or 2⁵/₈ inches as opposed to the 2¾-inch shell that's standard today. I'd consider no American Damascus gun safe with nitro powder unless you were willing to go to the expense and difficulty of sending it to England for nitro proof. And that's just *that*.

Blackpowder? I am not advising you to shoot it; even if I had seen your gun, I wouldn't considering the penalties for being wrong. But *I* would shoot modest, original-strength, original-chamber-length blackpowder loads through any high-quality, absolutely unpitted Damascus gun.

And study old books carefully for original loads before you ever start. Your left hand is even less replaceable than an antique Parker.

And what are the rewards? In England today, where they know that Damascus can be safe to shoot, the prices commanded by fine examples are very high. You can pay $2000 to $4000 for very good, shootable London Bests with the braided tubes. Of course, this is still less than the $40,000 and up for a new Best!

There are some real bargains around in the United States. It has been said of fine double guns that "the good ones are too expensive and the cheap ones aren't worth a damn." Often this is true, but it is not true of Damascus guns...at least not *yet*. If you are willing to be a scholar, if you feel the presence of earlier generations and the craftsman's love of his work revealed in his efforts a century after his death, if your eye responds to beauty and your hands to the feel of a fine bird gun, if you, like me and most other hunters, can only stand appalled at guns that cost as much as a house, then you might find there's still a lot of life in the old brown guns...

There are a lot of easily hidden faults in secondhand guns. Some are obvious. Don't buy guns with pitted barrels, L.C.s with cracked stocks, Parkers that have their actions blued where they should be case-hardened. Others are insidious. Don't take anybody's word for chamber length, unless you know a given model had chambers of a certain length. It's not that dealers are sleazy; most simply don't know. If you are buying an American shotgun and the barrels are other than 26-, 28-, 30-, or 32-inches (34 for Parker 8-gauges), look at the barrel ends for signs of cutting. A few were custom made at other lengths, but the chances are against it, especially in field-grade guns. Continental guns often have barrels a little more than 25 or a little less than 28 inches — metric measures. English and Spanish barrels are often 25 inches long — Churchill's influence.

On shotguns again — take off the forend, turn the gun upside down, and shake. Does it rattle? Not good — the barrels are loose at the hinge. No? Now — if you can do it without dropping the barrels on the floor, which the dealer will not appreciate — thumb the lever over to open while holding the barrels and shake again. Still tight? Good. Take the barrels off and look at the lumps. Do you see little dents or craters punched into the sides of the lump? Very bad — some butcher has peened the lump to tighten the action, an easy, sleazy, and extremely temporary repair. Forget this gun.

Now sight down the outside of the barrels. Look toward a window or some other mild light source so that you cast a line of light down the length of the barrel. Rotate the barrel so that this line plays over its entire surface. Look for dips or interruptions. These indicate dents — fixable, but a source of trouble if you neglect them. What is concave on the outside of the barrel is convex on the inside. Every time you fire a gun with a dent, you'll remove some metal, until you wear a hole in the barrel.

On rifles, try the safety test. Minor exterior barrel imperfections are less important — most rifle barrels are thick enough to guard against superficial denting, and length, even if altered, is less crucial to balance. Make sure everything moves smoothly but not so sloppily that it rattles. Check the bore for rifling wear. On rifles of heavy caliber, take the metal out of the stock (ask the dealer first!) and look for cracks in the wood.

And of course the minor fault that I've forgotten is probably the first one that will turn up in your gun.

And, well, so what? "Discovery, not acquisition, is what collecting, and life, is about," remember? Above all, try to have fun. You will lose money sometimes; you'll also acquire, with any luck, a treasure, a useful object built better than virtually anything else in our time. Good guns are expensive, relatively, even at the low end. But what the hell: cars rot and crash and even if they don't, are worth nothing in five years; furniture — and a true collector's gun — sits and collects dust; even the finest paintings, however wonderful when you buy them, often hang on the wall until, through familiarity, they turn into wallpaper. You go with your good gun into another world, to walk and breathe and stalk, to shoot with skill and grace and trained reflexes. The longer you have it, the better your gun will feel. Can you say that about any other tool, or work of art?

Let me insert a cautionary note.

Some of us spend our lives trading madly, always looking for The Perfect Gun. Unless we are very rich, the more we learn, the further perfection recedes. The habit of trading itself may make us rush straight past real perfection, realizing a trade or two down the line that we actually might have possessed what we "needed"— I'm not sure that's the verb that applies, except deep in the gut, but that's the one I use — and sent it on its way. A few of us are even shameless enough to try to get it back.

I am haunted by a few things here. One is the remark of my old gun-trading mentor in Cambridge, Massachusetts, who told me that you had to "blow" — his word — "at least $20,000 before you know a damn thing." Another is a line of writer Tony Atwill's: "I could turn a matched pair of Purdeys into a Mossberg pump in two trades."

10

One Good Gun

I have looked over your shoulder as you shopped for a shotgun*
and given you some advice of the kind that you might get if you
were just rambling through the rack. Now, let's get serious. I'll
deal with a few more of the choices you must make, and then show
you what all English and Continental sportsmen seem to learn
before they ever buy a gun: *You have to make your gun your own.*

Choices. First, gauge. I meant everything I said about loving
16s. But what do *you* shoot at? It's hard to fault a "light" — under
6½ pound — 12, for anything, or, rather, for everything. There are
more possible loads available for 12-gauge guns, even if we confine
ourselves to 2¾-inch loads. If you buy English, 2½-inch loads are
almost as diverse. (The 3-inch 12 is a specialist wildfowl and turkey
weapon and therefore a poor candidate for a generalist's one-gun
battery; American-style 3-inch "general" 12s like the Browning

*Rifles are more diverse and differ more from quarry to quarry. I
can't tell you which single rifle you must use, but I can give you some
ideas on which shotgun.

BSS are a bit too heavy for me.) If you shoot at everything, you can't go wrong with a 12; its only possible disadvantage is that it's a bit heavier than other alternatives, but at 6½ pounds, this will only be a problem if you run up and down hills all day, hunt in the heat, and/or have arthritis.

All the above apply to me, so I have a slight preference for the 16. I certainly wouldn't turn down a perfect 12, but at its ideal "English" weight of slightly less than 6 pounds, the 16 is just a bit easier to carry and swing after a long day in the field. You don't give up much in hitting power, either, except at the top end — turkeys and geese and steel shot game.

Which is not to say that many geese and probably turkeys haven't been taken with the smaller gauge, either, just that you must be more careful with your shots. My father had to give up his 32-inch-barreled Winchester double in some crisis during the fifties, but carried on shooting winter black ducks and Canada geese with his Browning 16-bore and never complained. Of course, 16 steel loads are a bit wimpy, but more efficient (and less gun-damaging) non-toxic loads are coming. I shoot mostly upland birds — local quail, pheasant, and grouse in Montana, and grouse and woodcock when I'm lucky enough to get to New England. I find the 16 more than adequate for all these. (It's much more efficient than a light 20 on plains grouse and ringnecks, which are big, wild-flushing birds.) Bandtail pigeons are often far away and hard to kill, but my 16 is lighter to carry into their 7500-foot-plus altitude. For geese, I use my (specialist) magnum 12 Sauer.

The 20 is the first gauge where small size begins to be a problem. If it is a "proper" 20, it is very light, about 5½ pounds (you can't get this in most American guns, with the exception of some fine old Foxes), but it shouldn't shoot more than ⁷/₈ oz. of shot, and ¾ is even better. Such a gun is really too small for avian plains game, although it's a fine— maybe even the best— gauge for woods grouse and woodcock and (probably) bobwhite. When I lived in New England, the 20 was my gauge of choice; it never failed to kill when I "pointed it straight," even with light loads.

The 3-inch 20 is a foolish gun. If it's a lightweight, it will hit you in the face like Mike Tyson; why shoot a 12-gauge load from a

20, which handles it less efficiently? If the gun is heavy, it makes even less sense. You might (I won't) like the sometime extra capacity of a light 3-incher; you might be able to stand one or two shots with it per season. But is there any rational reason on earth to carry a 20 that weighs as much as a bigger bore? If you think a light 20 kicks too much, cut down on your load.

The 28. Aesthetically, it's a delight, especially with long barrels. Practically, it's okay, more an expert's gun (though for reasons of light recoil, a surprisingly good beginner's gun) than one for every shooter. It's too small for pheasants! (I know, Jack O'Connor shot a 28 at pheasants; it's still too small!) It's great for grouse but better for woodcock; I had an uncomfortable sense that I had to wring more necks — that is, had more wounded birds — when I spent a season shooting grouse with it than I did with my 20, whereas all woodcock came down dead. It may be the ultimate gun for bobwhite quail, the only reason that I hesitated giving that award to the 20. Western quail, especially blues, flush a little too wild for it to be quite the best choice for them.

It's also the ultimate cottontail rabbit gauge. Tell *that* to the snobs.

We won't mention .410s. They are toys. Ten-gauges obviously are for specialists, at least in breechloading guns. There are some vintage and even new muzzleloading 10 doubles that would make excellent all-around shotguns, if you're a black powder fan; some of the old ones weigh under 7 pounds and have amazingly mild recoil for all that, at least with appropriate loads.

Before we go any further with choice, we should look at the idea I mentioned earlier — you should make your gun your own. There are only a couple of things you cannot change about your gun: its gauge (actually you can, but it's mostly a bad idea) and its barrel length. You can shorten a barrel (bad idea) but not lengthen it. Now, listen: Everything else is optional. *Everything.*

I've spoken a bit about collecting. If you are a collector, you want to leave the gun alone; anything you do to it, however refined, even if it actually improves the gun, is likely to lower its "value," i.e., *what somebody else will pay you for it.* From here on in, we are going to assume that you are keeping your gun and want it to work for *you.* Mostly, we're assuming that it's a good but not

135

fantastically expensive gun — a provincial English boxlock, a pre-war Belgian, a basically sound American gun that you want to make more lively. Really, though, it could as well apply to a Purdey or Boss.

Something that never seems to penetrate the brain of the average U.S. shooter is that there is no such thing as a "standard" English gun. Every single one is different. If one returns to the maker five decades after it left and they intend to resell it, they will refurbish the inside. But they will also plan to lengthen, shorten, bend the stock, to craft new barrels, do anything and everything needed to make the gun fit its new owner. Should you be more snobbish than Purdey's?

I should add that this is not the exclusive province of the rich, either. Virtually every small shop in England that imports new English-style Spanish guns advertises that it will "fit" — i.e., cut, bend, modify — its guns to fit their new owners. Let us have no more residual snobbery about original guns!

A few more thoughts before we tackle specifics. Do go to a gunsmith who specializes in fine doubles, not somebody who tight-ens actions with a whack of a hammer on the hook, or who hot-blues the barrels and says "whoops" when they fall apart. I will not give a list — look in the better gun magazines for ads. Large old outfits such as Orvis, Griffin & Howe, and Briley (not too "old") are all reputable. Former English gunsmiths such as Kirk Merrington, Nick Makinson, and David Trevallion, custom makers like Steven Dodd Hughes, are ones that I have dealt with and who do good work. But I am not a reference service; there are many out there, and I wish to slight no one. Talk to them and make your own deci-sions.

I did mention changing gauges above. Some good gun-smiths can sleeve — more about this soon — your gun down to a smaller gauge. The trouble with this is that you inevitably end up with a thick breech area proportional to the barrels, and a gun that is heavy for the gauge — an expensive way to own an awkward gun. It's not the gunsmith's fault, either; I once briefly owned a 12-gauge Westley Richards (a gun I would not have bought if I had read this book first) with 16-gauge barrels fitted by *Westley Richards* to a 12-bore action. It handled like a log.

Okay, specifics. *BARRELS*. By now you know I like 28-inch barrels, or metric 27-and-a-bit, on Continental guns. I think longer is better than shorter, and I'm a shortish, stout Mediterranean, no string bean. Americans tend to prefer short barrels because their 28- and 30-inch barrels were heavy; their guns felt more lively with the short barrels. But long, light barrels swing more smoothly and make most people I know shoot better. For years I worked at this by trial and error; some guns just felt (and shot) better than others. I finally found the objective correlative in Datus Proper's *Pheasants of the Mind*. He quotes Gene Hill: "...virtually all 'good guns' have barrels that weigh...just about three pounds — regardless of whether they are twenty-six or thirty inches. Smaller gauges, twenties and twenty-eights, will of course weigh...less, but not much." Proper adds: "Don't go over three pounds for the uplands."

His formula works perfectly. The only double I shoot now with barrels that weigh more than three pounds is my magnum Sauer, a gun that is an eight-pound-plus monster. My current 16-gauge Darne's 27-and-a-bit barrels weigh only 2 pounds 8 ounces! And I once owned a beautiful Damascus Ingram from Scotland whose 30-inch tubes still weighed a hair under three pounds; it handled like a feather.

I *hate* most 25-inch barrels. The exceptions that I've seen have been Churchill sidelocks that cost more than a new car; they were built to balance.

Your own size matters some, too, especially if you are very tall. Datus Proper is built like Ichabod Crane; his lovely Woodward has a 16-inch stock and 29-inch barrels, and is as stout through the action as a live pigeon competition gun. Thomas McGuane's Chapman is another gun that looks more like a duck gun than an upland piece to me. Both these tall men have had the sense to have their guns made to fit them, not to some mythical average shooter.

I guess my feelings can be be summed up easily: Get long, light barrels if you can. Need I add that you don't have to cut barrels off to get open chokes?

SLEEVING. Curiously, this practice, quite common across the ocean, is not yet well-understood here. Most people confuse it with the addition of full-length tubes or lining to heavy skeet guns to allow them to shoot smaller-gauge shells.

Sleeving is more like re-barreling. The gunsmith cuts the barrels off just in front of the chambers and uses them as a monobloc to hold two new barrel tubes. The old ribs, upper and lower, are retained and re-fitted. The resulting barrels can be lighter than the old tubes, can have (slightly) different chamber lengths, different chokes, even (as described above) different gauges than the originals.

Sleeving is a good solution for severely damaged or pitted barrels; a good job, once blued, is virtually indistinguishable from a new set of barrels and is just as durable. What I hate is that it is becoming a common "remedy" for fine old Damascus guns because of our paranoia about their safety. If your Damascus gun has smooth, unpitted barrels that are still within proof dimensions (get your gunsmith to run a micrometer on them), do yourself and your heirs a favor and leave them alone, except for maybe a good rust-brown finish. Get or learn to build appropriate loads. Save sleeving for the basket cases. At a cost that begins at $700 as I write (1994), it's a bargain compared to the $5000-plus cost of new barrels.

CHOKE. I think nobody ever shot badly with improved cylinder. It's the most useful choke in the uplands, and not a bad one for decoying ducks. The range from tight improved to tight modified works best with steel; again, be aware that more lead-like non-toxics are coming.

One tighter choke is probably necessary for shooting on the plains, although I doubt its utility in thick grouse and woodcock cover. It's also an asset for the one-gun gunner. These days I prefer near cylinder in the right and almost full in the left — "a choice, not an echo." This is for 16- and 12-gauge guns; you'd want a bit more choke in the right for 20s and 28s.

I went through a brief fascination with choke tubes and have passed them by, at least for two-barreled hunting guns. I never changed them anyway. They can be good for sporting clays and may be necessary in utility single-barrels. I might yet put one in the left barrel of my Sauer; I don't use super-choke for wildfowl, but you can't be too tight for turkey. If there's no choke in your barrel, a gunsmith can add a little by cutting you a "jug choke" — a widened recess behind the muzzle that then narrows down again in the final inch. I doubt it's necessary, but then I like near-cylinder bores.

The easiest part of the gun to modify is the *STOCK*. First, though, make a rough test to see if you are going to need much modification. Look at a mark on the far wall and mount the gun quickly while looking at the mark; close your eyes while staring at the same mark, mount the gun, and open them; see where it points. George Bird Evans long ago made the suggestion that whether you shoot with your mouth closed or open can make a real difference. Clench your teeth and notice how (if you are right-handed) that action raises your head and moves it to the left of the stock. Do you know which you do?

Stock length. Most shooters have an idea of what they like. Many would shoot better with a longer stock, providing they learn to thrust the gun out when they mount it, especially in the uplands. The American standard length used to be between 14 and 14½ inches, measured from the front trigger to the center of the butt; now it seems to be moving out closer to what I'd call European standard, between 14¾ and 15 inches, perhaps a sign of increasing sophistication among shooters. Wildfowl guns are and *should* be shorter; you use them while wearing heavier clothes and, though this may be heretical, seem to "aim" them more.*

No matter how short you like your stock, make sure it's long enough so that your thumb does not contact your nose when you fire. Other short stock problems include cutting your thumb on the safety and banging your second finger on the trigger guard or your trigger finger when you pull the second. First triggers are often hinged to move forward, but all these signs indicate you should have a bit more stock length.

*If you think you need to shorten, go back and read my first remarks on that subject, and sleep on it. You will very rarely, if you are an American male, really need to shorten a stock. Female shooters are both shorter on the average and, obviously, built differently; many may need a slightly shorter stock, though they too should check first. Most women also can profit from a more rounded edge on the stock or recoil pad, especially on the lower inside surface, where it contacts their breast.

Stock

Height of Comb. First, find out where you hit. Bob Brister suggested the easiest method. Take a bed sheet and tack it up on a frame at the distance you usually take your first shot — say, 25 yards or less. Draw a bird's bold outline at its center with a magic marker. Return to your mark, load up with small shot (to make the pattern denser), and begin to fire at the "bird." Do not aim, or mount your gun and then fire, but mount and fire instantly as the gun touches your shoulder. Use both barrels. In a little while — less than a box of shells — you'll make a distinct, if ragged, hole in the sheet at the natural center of your pattern. This is where your gun shoots.

Is the hole to one side of the bird? Above it, or below? Shooting to one side must be corrected, but a high-shooting gun can be an advantage — it provides a little "built-in-lead" for rising birds. Personally, I like it. I can't think of any situation that would be improved by a low-shooting gun, but probably someone will write to me and let me know what it is.

Now, what can you do about it if the point of impact is off? There are a few easy home remedies that will be effective but may need some refinishing for cosmetic reasons — again, see below — and a menu of alterations that gunsmiths, including ones that you might not want to do more sophisticated work, can accomplish.

Incorrect height and shooting to one side, if they are slight, can be affected by minor sanding of the comb. Put a little shaving cream under your cheekbone and see where your cheek contacts the stock. Then wrap a piece of *fine* — say, 220 grit — wet-and-dry sandpaper around a rectangular rubber eraser and sand *with the grain*. This will almost inevitably make a mark so much lighter than the original finish that you will have to replace it all, but don't despair; you can do that at home, too. Go *very* slowly. Heed my italics.

Butt. The prettiest stocks have simple checkered wood butts, although some find them too slippery. The second nicest looking butt treatment (other than such esoterica as skeleton butts and heel-and-toe plates) is a smoothly rounded "English"style, i.e., solid, recoil pad. Pachmayr makes them in red and black and in several thicknesses; although some dealers say that a real English Silvers brand pad adds more value, I suspect that's a bit of Anglophile snobbery; both look fine, and the Pachmayr costs less. I think the color is a matter of choice; I prefer red on brightly colored, highly figured stocks, and black on dark ones; again, some claim that red is more "English."

You can now get pads with recoil-eating, jellylike synthetic rubber interiors. They are probably more practical than checkered butts, and you can either add them to shortened stocks, to finish them, or use them for a little extra length. Any gunsmith can install one, though a good one makes them fit more smoothly. You can smooth the edges down yourself with fine sandpaper (wet) and maybe a bit of soft steel wool.

Other options include leather-covered pads — a bit impractical and high-maintenance, but pretty and available only from high-end gunsmiths — and wooden stock extensions. These can be matched amazingly well to the existing grain by *really* good (and well-supplied) gunsmiths, and are the only way to go if you want to keep a checkered or skeleton buttplate. They have the advantage of being available at any length (recoil pads stop at about an inch) but are expensive and never match 100%. They can approach 90%, though....

Cast-off or on. You don't want to do this at home, though some have tried. Until recently most Americans shot shotguns with absolutely straight (from left to right) stocks and considered "cast" — a stock that bends slightly to the right for a right-handed shooter or left for a left-handed one, bringing his face directly in line behind the barrels — a weird habit more suited to decadent or rich Europeans. Personally, I hate to shoot a gun without it. I have a very broad face and tend to shoot to one side with any gun that features a straight, well-rounded comb.

Most European guns you buy will have some, probably enough, cast *off* — i.e., right-hander's cast. But if you shoot off your left shoulder or are adapting an American gun, you might want to consider bending your stock.

Bending— which is also a good method of adjusting a stock up or down — usually consists of immersing the stock in very hot linseed oil, then bending it (to a point slightly beyond the desired configuration, as wood tends to spring back a bit when it dries.

The process sounds messy, but works very well. It is not cheap, and the gunsmiths who do it will generally not guarantee that the wood will not break. This sounds scarier than it is. I have never heard of a gun accepted for alterations breaking. One gunsmith who does such work says firmly that he has never had one break. The alteration is permanent, and the surface needs refinishing.

There's a rumor out that some are now bending stocks after microwaving them. I can see how it could work theoretically, but I haven't tried it. I've owned guns bent by the hot-oil process, shot several more, seen it done once, and watched a video of it several times. It's a tried and true process, and it works.

Oh, and *dominant eyes*. If you shoot off your right shoulder and have a left-dominant eye, you may be a re-trained lefty. You will then either have to consider a severely bent stock; learning to shoot off your left shoulder; or— the easiest— learning to trick your dominant eye. A "spot" of paint or piece of tape floating in your shooting glasses lens can mask your cominant eye long enough to let the other take over. My late partner Betsy Huntington chose this expedient and shot very well.

This may be the place to address *balance*, too, if only for a moment. If your gun is too barrel-heavy, you can put lead, such as fishing sinkers, in the stock while the pad is off. Often there are already holes there, and you can make the sinkers fit snugly with a bit of cloth or paper toweling. Weight too close to the butt has always seemed awkward to me, and besides, you can also have plugs removed by a competent gunsmith from the rear of a gun with a checkered butt in order to bore holes and lighten or add lead. Don't do this lightly.

A cruder option to *add* weight forward is to wrap a little lead foil around the barrels or under a slip-on hand guard. I'd rather choose a gun that fit in the first place; going this way risks making your gun look as patchy as that of your average small-town trap-shooter. Rubber (as in recoil pads) is usually heavier than wood.

If you are still in the choosing stage: ejectors, because they have more metal, make marginally heavier forends than extractors. And I suppose you (not I) could always add a beavertail up there for more weight....

Refinishing: these days, I almost always refinish my own stocks, thanks to the advice of David Simpson. I can't checker, but I can do 'most anything else; if you go slowly and carefully, and (or) mask the checkering with tape, you can generally avoid hurting it. If it's already flat and damaged, hire it out and do the rest yourself. What follows is a general plan. Go slowly. All stock woods are a little different; all stocks pose different problems.

Some theory first. Most people who are not stockmakers do not realize that even magnificently figured stocks are often "colored," that is, stained. Figure in itself does not guarantee color. The classic reddish color in old English guns comes from alkanet root. (A version called Purdey's Warthog Finish is available these days, recommended by Ross Seyfried; I haven't used it yet.) I have had good luck with substances as humble as Ace Hardware's Special Walnut stain. (You want the penetrating oil version, not the one with varnish.) David Simpson has brewed up a version with cherry and mahogany stains mixed with thinner. You get the idea.

Next: the classic stock finish is linseed oil. Nothing else seems to give quite the depth and luster and richness. However, pure or near-pure linseed is dark and tends never quite to dry. In reaction, many commercial gunmakers have gone to horrible shiny plastic shell finishes, or more sophisticated hard dry matte-surfaced compositions that look like oil and are extremely durable but rather dull, without oil's depth and luster. Nor are most of these finishes easily repaired by rubbing in a drop of oil, as are the classic ones.

What follows is a labor-intensive method that combines most of the virtures of the old and new. You'll stain, sand, polish, rub in oil, and seal a durable, beautiful, low-maintenance finish. I'm going to quote from a letter of David's, and interpolate my own comments.

Materials list

varnish remover (like "Stryp-Eez")
garnet or silicon oxide sandpaper, 150 grit
220 grit wet- or dry- sandpaper
320 grit wet or dry sandpaper
rubber eraser (school type)
masking tape
boiled linseed oil
Tru oil or Lin-Speed oil
    stain — any of the above or mahogany stain from Garret Wade,
    N.Y.C., Les Produits de les Ancien Ebenists brand foam brushes
    (small)
000 steel wool
soft cotton cloth
tack rag
paste wood filler, walnut colored (for open-pored woods only)
pumice powder
3M scouring pad

First, remove the old finish with the stripper. It's best to remove as much metal as possible from the stock before you start, although if you are careful, you can work around it and use the metal for a "handle." If I leave the metal on, I mask it with the tape, cutting it to shape with a small, sharp knife. You'll probably have to use a lot of steel wool, something to scrape, *and* a tooth-brush (for the checkering) to get the finish off. This is the messiest and least-pleasant part of the whole process.

To quote David, "Any reshaping should be done now, using rasps, files, or coarse sandpaper." *With* the grain! If you do this, mask the checkering first.

"If only refinishing, begin sanding with 220 grit paper, making sure *not* to sand the wood to a level below that of any metal parts.

"Using 220 (or 150 if necessary), sand wood and recoil pad to flush meeting, *using eraser as a sanding pad.*" (This keeps you from making dents or low spots.) "Don't spare paper!

"The quality of your sanding will affect the final outcome *dramatically.* Go slowly and carefully, keeping all flat surfaces flat, curves rounded, etc.

"The goal of sanding is to remove scratches, so work up through 320 grit, making sure that all visible scratches are removed, along with dents and imperfections."

(If you have a small dent, you can often raise it by dampening it, covering it with a wet cloth, and applying a hot iron for a moment. Don't force it.)

"Wet entire stock with water, and dry rapidly with a hair dryer or flame to raise the grain of the wood." The surface will now feel a bit rough — "whiskery" — to your fingers. "Cut off fuzz with 320 grit sandpaper." Remember to keep the paper wrapped around that eraser! "Repeat."

"Using stain full strength and foam brush, cover the stock with an even coat of stain." Stroke the brush briskly from one end of the stock to the other. The idea is to get an even coat of color, without overlaps. Keep going until it's a bit darker than you think you want. David adds, "Two coats are usually sufficient; dry fully between coats." If you are staining a stock with an addition of a different wood, you might have to give one piece more stain than the other.

"If grain is raised slightly during staining, cut whiskers with a light rubbing of 000 steel wool. Wipe down stock with tack rag to remove any steel particles."

Carefully mask the checkering, cutting along the edges with an Exacto or other small, sharp knife. It's a pain, but worth the trouble.

"With your hands, rub in a generous coat of linseed oil, which should soak fully into wood. Let dry two days. Make sure *all* oil is rubbed into the wood. Do not allow it to dry on the surface." Once you have done this, it becomes second nature. You rub until your hands generate heat, and the oil just sucks into the surface. After the first few coats, it goes more slowly, and the two-day drying period becomes necessary.

"Repeat until wood reaches desired darkness and richness. Allow the final coat to dry for [at least] four days.

"If the grain of the wood needs filling, apply paste filler and remove according to instructions — one or two coats. Remove the excess with 3M scouring pad." Most European walnuts will not need this step, although it's worth remembering for old American rifles and such.

"Attach stock to holding fixtures." (Not necesary, but it makes things easier!) "Apply Tru-oil (or Lin-Speed) with the grain, smoothing on this coat, attempting to minimize unevenness or streaks. Work on a small area of the stock at a time, rubbing gently until the finish begins to dry under your hand. If a section dries before it is completely smooth and level, add a *bit* more finish on the tips of your fingers and recover. Continue until the entire stock has an even coat."

This is the sealing coat — it's hard and durable and, when it dries, not sticky. It preserves the rich oil coat underneath. "Let it dry one or two hours in warm weather, longer in cool." David is in south Texas and I'm in New Mexico. If you live in a cool, damp climate, overnight is best.

"Apply at least three coats, rubbing lightly between drycoats with triple-0 steel wool, cleaning up with the tack rag. Allow the final coat to dry a full *five days.*

"Make a paste of linseed [not Tru or Lin-Speed] oil and pumice." This should be a little stiffer than, say, maple syrup; if too dry, add oil; if too wet, pumice.

"Using felt or a cotton sheet or shirt stretched over the eraser, rub gently with the grain, polishing the finish and removing any lap marks or unevenness. Rub only hard enough to polish and achieve an even, semi-gloss finish. Remove all grit and polish with a soft cloth.

"When it's dry, put a drop of linseed on the stock and rub completely into the wood, covering the entire surface with a *very* thin coat. The entire stock should look wet and glossy. Allow to dry at least two days before handling." Strip the tape off.

Stain the checkering, if you need to, and brush in one coat of linseed with a toothbrush. You're done.

The one thing I'd emphasize twice: *Go slowly.* I tend toward impatience. But I've found that many coats of linseed are better than a few, and many days drying beats hurrying. You'll be glad you went slowly, believe me.

There are a few more things you can do to make your gun truly yours. *Trigger pulls* are almost infinitely malleable. I like mine light. Most English guns are fine; many Continental ones, including Darne's, are rather heavy. Do go to a *good* gunsmith for this one, though; improperly hardened sears can wear rapidly and go off unexpectedly.

The opposite problem can exist in old guns, too: dangerously light trigger pulls, even ones that go off when you pull the other trigger. One way to test them, though not infallable, is to put on the safety, pull the trigger hard, and then ease the safety off. If the hammer then fails, do not fire the gun until you have had the trigger fixed. Of course, some dangerous triggers won't reveal themselves this easily. Do I have to remind the readers of this book never to point their guns in an unsafe direction, even for one lazy moment?

Loose actions. The old cliché about loose, rattling actions when I was growing up was that they were "shot out." They are *not.* Even if a gun is "off the face," loose both laterally and vertically, it can usually be fixed by the addition of a new (slightly oversized) hinge pin and, possibly, new metal to the sides of the lumps. The price of this operation starts these days at only $350. A gun that is loose laterally — when you wiggle it from side-to-side — is probably still quite safe to shoot, though it's not going to get any tighter.

(This, by the way, is another operation for a double gun specialist. Many country gunsmiths will, as I mentioned, peen the sides of the lump or bang on the hook. These are not competent or permanent methods of tightening your action!)

Case hardening, bluing, etcetera....the metal surface finish. These are the last things you should consider... your gun shoots perfectly well without them and may well look better as an "antique" than as a shiny new gun!

Good bluing — soft, cold, rust bluing — is an improvement. It's not cheap, and a job for a specialist. I *hate* a bright, shiny-blue finish; it's out-of-place on a classic double.

If you have *any* trace of case-colors, I'd leave the surface alone. If they are gone, there are a few outfits that will harden your gun's surface with dark, rich, durable case-colors. These, and maybe the so-called "French gray" surface, are the only metal finishes that enhance the look of a fine double. I can't get used to coin-finished actions (although some old guns wear to a near-coin finish that is attractive). Even Parker's original colors seem a little garish, a little too much toward the orange end of the spectrum. I have seen one Parker and one L.C. that have been redone in English-type colors, and they looked wonderful.

Case-coloring does involve heat (and old bones and cyanide and, for all, I know, Voodoo) and may slightly warp thin metal like lockplates. Sometimes an action will gape a little on the face after a new case-hardening, although this can be fixed. One good company refused to color one of my Darnes because they weren't sure just how that weird action would warp. I forgave them. Listen to your gunsmith!

A few old English and Continental guns, especially sidelocks, were made with a plain black surface decorated only by border engraving. Such guns, called "Black Widow" guns, are surprisingly attractive. The legend (probably not true) is that they were made for widows, or widowers. They have the advantage of being very easy to refinish, too! I once had one with the nicest wood of any gun I have ever owned.

An oval or crest-shaped stock plate for your initials is an attractive grace note if your gun already has one. They are not cheap, even in silver, if you are adding one; having your monogram engraved is cheap enough if one already exists.

One reason that English guns last forever is that the owners send them in at the end of the season for inspection and deep cleaning. Potential problems can be anticipated: flat springs replaced, trigger pulls adjusted, swelled wood sanded down, cracks filled. A few English-trained gunsmiths now offer this service in the U.S. and it's spreading. If you get a good old gun, it's a good idea to send it off for inspection immediately, for an estimate of what it needs and what you can let slide or do yourself. After that, a yearly or bi-annual "tuneup" isn't a bad idea.

Of course, if you have the dollars, you can just go out and buy a Purdey or a Holland. If I had a million, I 'd go to Dickson or McKay Brown and order a 16-bore round action. Trouble is, it would cost me my last three year's income! Instead, I'll get a good old boxlock that will give me 95% of the aesthetics of that gun at one tenth the price, and adapt it to suit me. I'll find and polish my own diamond in the rough.

Believe me: If I can find, and afford, one good gun, *anyone* can. Good luck, and good shooting.

Appendix I:

The Illustrated Gun

Malcolm Appleby, Scottish master engraver, has a credo and a profession as old as mankind: "to create," as he writes in a letter, " a totem object that is personal to the user. This engraving may have no connection with shooting but...helps to create a unique functional object that is powerful enough in design to be its master's mascot." Appleby is the latest and possibly the most outspoken of the oldest kind of artist, the maker of hunter's tools.

Humans have not only always hunted, they have always created beautiful functional objects, some of the them hunting weapons, in which aesthetics were as important as function. And sometimes *more* important; some of the perfectly symmetrical laurel-leaf points crafted by the Paleo-Indians of Clovis, New Mexico, more than 10,000 years ago were more beautiful than useful, as delicate as jewelry. As soon as any hunting tool existed, someone made a decorative version. Spears and swords used in medieval Europe for hunting boar were made with elaborately engraved hunting scenes and inlays of precious metal. As soon as the gun came on the scene, it too received the attention of artisans.

The perception of guns as purely utilitarian, even ugly, objects would be alien to all the old gunmaking cultures. Embellished firearms were popular among Islamic raiders, Kentucky woodsmen, German boar hunters, Japanese samurai, and English wildfowlers. Craftsmen carved stocks and inlaid them with ivory and staghorn, gold and silver, and rare woods.

They began to chisel and cut designs into the iron, to etch patterns into it with acid while protecting the rest of the surface with wax. In the words of museum curator Irene Grabowska, "Firearms began to take on a 'status' role that often overshadowed their purpose." The inlaid gun reached its highest — or perhaps it most decadent — point in the so-called Napoleon guns of the French gunmaker Lepage. Made from about 1805 to 1810 as presentation arms for Napoleon I, they are double-barreled flintlocks decorated with carved faces and so much gold and silver that it would seem impossible to hold them comfortably, let alone hunt with them.

In England, the gun evolved differently. The English never lost track of function. English gunmakers paid more attention to graceful stocks and strong, hard walnut than to gold inlays. Their guns were always functional and, to an educated eye, perhaps held more beauty than the jewel-encrusted monstrosities from the Continent. Meanwhile, in the area around Brescia in northern Italy, craftsmen were perfecting the tools and techniques of engraving. Brescian engravers became the world's finest. Today they use not only the hammer-driven scriber, the universal engraver's tool, but also the graver, or *bulino*. The engraver holds the bulino with his right hand only. It provides the control and detail of a fine pen or pencil and has enabled the Italian engravers to produce, on metal, game scenes of photographic realism and detail.

There are other national "schools" of engraving. Some, like the German and Austrian deep-relief carvings, have survived to this day. German engraving has a lot in common with the old

Continental style. It is heavy, rather stylized, given to oak leaves and chunky beasts at bay, and ignores for the most part the firearm as a whole. The Germans also tend to carve the gunstock.

Another minor "school" is that of guns made by English makers for eastern provinces. These guns — Holland & Holland and Westley Richards made magnificent examples in the late 19th century — combine English shape and utility with elaborate arabesque scrolls and inlays in ivory and gold. English makers still build such guns for the oil sheikhs. Some have the kind of art nouveau flowers and loops favored by the Indian princes; others depict sports practiced in Arabia, such as falconry..

English- and Italian-style double guns and American rifles, in which function and elegance are blended, are probably today's finest examples of the gun as art, though they are all quite different.

In England, the really great guns are now priced out of reach of all but a handful of the richest shooters. Men of impeccably conservative British taste buy the standard Purdey "rose and scroll" design, an unobtrusive yet difficult-to-execute pattern that hasn't changed since Theophilus Murcott put the hammers inside sidelocks. It is the equivalent of a Savile Row suit or, as Malcolm Appleby says, "like an old school tie. You choose your gun to show where in shooting society you would wish to belong."

Lately, Holland & Holland, which always was a little less stuffy than Purdey, has attempted to break away from the ultraconservative "dress" of the West End double. Holland employs Ken Hunt, the only Englishman featured in Mario Abbiatico's work on engraving, who is master of realistic animals and birds.

Italian guns are even more flamboyant. Their shape and mechanical works owe a lot to English concepts and patents, but their embellishment is heavily influenced by their own Renaissance art. At its best, in shotguns made by such top-of-the-line makers as Fabbri or Famars (Abbiatico and Salvinelli), the marriage of English and Italian ornament is a fortuitous one. Such guns feature gorgeous wood, quick-pointing, racy lines, and lockwork resembling fine watches. They also cost as much as a good car. Great Italian engravers include Firmo Fracassi, who has done work in deep-relief baroque style as well as in bulino, Angelo Galeazzi, and Gianfranco Pedersoli.

Although some aficionados may damn me for saying so, American makers have never built or embellished double guns quite fine enough to compete on the international level. Parker's birds and dogs never reached Italian standards, nor its scroll the English. L.C. Smith's gold lightning bolts are best ignored. But American bolt rifles have reached a level that in my opinion exceed the best ever achieved, even by such high-end English firms as Holland & Holland.

Such guns are always built by individual gunmakers such as Jerry Fisher or Dale Goens, or small shops such as Griffin & Howe, on classic actions like the pre-'64 Model 70 Winchester or the Mauser. Their inletting is as good as anything in England. If you take the action out of the stock in a rifle made by a great American stocker, it will look as though the wood grew around the metal. Their checkering, both in quality and design, and their detailing exceed anything done in Europe for at least 200 years. Finally, their stocks are sensibly shaped. They are high enough at the comb for shooting with scope sights — no small achievement if you look at them alongside contemporary English rifle stocks. (Even those by the best tend to have low combs or lumpy cheek-pieces.)

Lately, the finest exhibition work by the greats has evolved almost to the point of decadence again. It is a very fine line, and one can celebrate the craftsmanship of such guns. But a master-work such as the Holland Saurian — a double 4-bore entirely covered with bas-relief dinosaurs, with lizard-skin recoil pad, petrified sponge crest plate, pterodactyls on the fences, and an exhibition case full of fossil bones — is almost as excessive as the creatures it celebrates. Far worse is the attitude of some collectors (though it would take a strong-minded, very rich man to lug the Saurian double 4 out to the salt marshes). A friend, a stockmaker, overheard at a gun show a conversation that covered "responsibility," "cultural history," and, inevitably, "*investment*." One of the collectors informed the company that he would never hunt with or even fire, his fine guns.

Which is why I come back to Malcolm Appleby with some relief. Appleby is an inspired eccentric who engraves entire guns as single animals — a woodcock, a crocodile, a pike. His craftsmanship is above criticism, his designs unique in the history of firearms.

His details amaze: A single gold scale forms the safety on the pike gun; the bird's eyes glare from the fences of the woodcock gun, its foot is the lower tang, and the landscape peeps from beneath its outspread wings on the sidelocks..

It isn't just Appleby's designs that are a departure from tradition.   His attitude is, too. He worked for years for David McKay Brown, a Scottish gunmaker who builds guns on the graceful yet functional Dickson-style "round" action, a design in which there isn't a single unnecessary line. Who buys them?   To quote Appleby again, "Round actions sell well in Scotland to people who use rather than merely collect guns...I am trying in my own sweet way to create an identity perhaps for the individualist who is not concerned with an establishment peer group."

I like that. I like to think, not of Scotsmen necessarily, but of the American shotgunner who traditionally hunts with an old friend — an individual who isn't out to prove his social position by the classicism of his gun. How about a raccoon gun? An alligator? How about a peregrine falcon, its feathers hard and shining?

One of my minor objectives in visiting London last year was to see an example of Appleby's work. In 1985, the Royal Armoury of the Tower of London commissioned Appleby to create, on a McKay Brown action, its first modern piece. Given the raven mascots of the Tower, what more appropriate theme for their gun than that of a raven?

We may have been the only visitors on that bright May day to care about the Raven gun, and finding it took some searching. We finally discovered it in a dimly lit case in a darker corner of the Armoury, behind an annoyingly reflective pane of glass. (Write to the Tower and complain!) But even in such unfavorable circumstances, it looked eerily animate, almost breathing. I was reminded of a remark by Becky Gray, one of the former owners of *Gray's Sporting Journal*: When I showed her a photo of an Appleby gun, she exclaimed in awe, " It's like *God* made it." The surface of the gun's action was browned and case-hardened, covered with feathers so three-dimensional and "soft" that it seemed impossible that they were metal. You felt that if a breeze had dared stir in that glass-cased mausoleum, it would ruffle the gun's feathers. And yet the overall gun had the sweeping functional lines of a working

English game gun, one that should be allowed to do its work, to prey on incoming grouse on a cold moor. Was it only me, or was it a minor crime that it should be stuck on this dusty museum, like a dog in a city apartment? Appleby's design put Neolithic magic back into hunters' tools, explicitly.

Engraved Lockplate

Appleby may be the most inspired designer in the world, but he claims that others have more skill as craftsmen. Perhaps the finest of these is an American, Winston Churchill. If you drive into Proctorsville in central Vermont, you enter an older part of the state, one not yet full of vaction ski homes, condos, and what my Montana friend John Barsness calls "fake pickups for yuppies."

Winston Churchill, though he engraves fine guns by Fabbri of Italy and Purdey's of London, is true Vermont as apple pie for breakfast. He lives in a house across the street from where he was born (the old house burned down when he was a child). Behind his house the hill slopes steeply down to a little stream, then rises into a slanting pasture that is a natural backdrop for a couple of rifle targets. I felt as though I were back home in rural New Mexico when he explained that it was possible to test rifles at marked distances from the windows of his workshop. I use my backyard in Magdalena as a firing range but, after six months of exile in the Northeast, had practically forgotten that anyone else did so.

I already knew a little of Churchill's background. He had grown up artistically talented in Proctorsville; had started working on such projects as stocking rifles; and finally, becoming fascinated with engraving, had taken a portfolio of his work to crusty old Joe Fugger, Abercrombie & Fitch's legendary master engraver (and the only person before Churchill who was ever honored by having an in-the-white Purdey shipped overseas to engrave).

Fugger gave him some cautious encouragement, and he was off. Now, twenty years later, he has combined the best of several traditional styles. Like German and Austrian engravers, he constructs fully rounded, often inlaid animals. Like the English, he is a master of scroll, though unlike them he dislikes having it all of one size. Like the Italians, he does almost photographic background work. But his can fade back delicately, leaving the figures standing boldly in the foreground. His overall effect is unique; one might call it American classic, though he is really the only one who does it so well.

Churchill got out his 35mm camera to take photos of my springers and falcon as I exercised them after the long drive to his home. Everything is grist for the mill: "Who knows" he said. "Someday you may see them on a gun."

What did he have around? "I'm only working on one project at the moment — I hope you can see something from it. It's a little Purdey."

Upstairs in the workshop, everything was neat, bright, almost antiseptic. Rows of art books, a few drawings, and Churchill's own set of working guns — an old Simson of Suhl 16-gauge, an heirloom Parker goose gun, a few rifles — completed the decor. No Purdeys?

He grinned. "I can't afford my own work."

The Purdey was a slender, shallow-framed Woodward-patent over-under in 28-gauge. Even in the white, with only the borders done on the locks, it was the kind of gun that could give a fine-gun fanatic a fierce case of the I-*must*-have-one's. Churchill had carved out the leaflike designs on the fences and a few panels of scroll. There was a large space in the center of each lock where the scene would go. But even here it was easy to see that there would be spaces of unengraved metal to set it all off. I pointed this out, and he agreed.

"*Contrast*," he stated. "That's what makes us see things. I hate seeing all small scroll with no space or contrast. If you look at those scrolls, you'll see that they are proportion — finer in some areas than in others. And the 'tendrils' get finer toward the extremities." All of these effects are quite intentional; what the observer sees is a harmony made up of those contrasts.

Better was to come. He took the finished trigger guard out of its drawer. On it, three gold woodcock flushed and towered toward an opening above. He handed me a magnifying glass. Each woodcock was as perfect as a fine painting. Steel showed between the golden toes of each foot, between every splayed primary. The eyes looked dark and liquid, with a glinting highlight in each. The background was soft, as it would appear if you were focused on a rising bird, not hard-edged and distracting. As I peered through the glass, Churchill quietly extended a wooden match into my field of view. Its head was twice the size of the smallest 'cock.

He showed me a few photos. One set was of an Italian Fabbri, an over-under not unlike the Purdey. On the locks was a pair of gold Brittany spaniels.

"Remember what I said when I took the pictures of your dogs? Those dogs are both my old Brit."

I couldn't believe the contrasts in the dogs, the obvious dark spots on a light background. Did he use two colors of gold?

"No. Just chisels and shading."

The dogs were *alive*. Few engravers I have ever seen understand anatomy as well as Churchill does; he is far ahead of the great Italian engravers in this respect.

He spoke of technique. "I usually don't encourage people to watch, 'cause they get bored. It looks like I'm sitting there, doing nothing. The motions are too small.

"When I'm stippling, I actually lift a piece of metal out each time. But you can't see me do it. It's like the old quick-draw joke: 'Want to see my quick-draw? Want to see it again?'"

He took out a piece of paper and drew a sketch to show me how he undercuts the steel to hold a gold inlay, then chisels tiny channels into the bottom of the inlay cut and undercuts *them*. And how it's necessary to make smooth cuts when you are working on the microscopic primaries of an inlaid woodcock. "Some engravers get wavy lines — it doesn't look right."

We disagreed, mildly, on the use of engraved arms in the field. I felt they ought to be given their day out, even it it's only a bright, sunny day in a quail field. He understood my attitude — "That's because you're a user. You use your own guns. But these guys who commission this kind of work already have enough guns to shoot. They want these to hang like paintings." The reluctance of a collector to take out a piece on which the engraving alone goes well into five figures is understandable, I guess. It should be noted that Churchill — who really can't afford his own work — uses his own shooters every day in the field, and is a man after my own heart.

A final anecdote that might illustrate one aspect of his genius is that much-referred-to (and rarely seen) infinite capacity for taking pains. As I was going, and after listening to him on technique, I mentioned the highlight in that half-matchhead-sized woodcock's eye.

"I bet I know how you did that. You chiseled up a little point of gold out of the eye and raised it up...."

"Yes...and then I burnished it."

Appendix II:

My Guns

In the first *Good Guns* I called this appendix "My Guns — Present and Future," which now sounds pretty smug. I've taken a more relaxed attitude toward exactly what I have these days. For one thing, I don't have enough money to have everything I think I "need," not really enough to fill all my ecological gun niches. For a second thing, I have realized that my opinions change.

One thing that increasing age (and wisdom?) has done for me is that, unless the need is very real and not merely some variation of "want," I'd rather go temporarily without rather than own something second-rate. On the other hand, "second-rate" and "in need of repair" are two different things. I'll sometimes buy something old and fine, even if it needs work, if I know it's basically sound.

I'd like to repeat something I said in the first edition for this chapter. It still makes sense: "It seems that a reader should have some idea what this opinionated writer shoots. Does he follow his own advice? Can he afford to? Or does he advise against collecting and yet own fifty guns?"

Shotguns. Obviously, there's always a Darne. I still dream about a "light" 10 owned by a friend in England. Can't afford it yet....

I have reclaimed my father's old Sweet Sixteen Browning autoloader as a dove and light "steel" duck gun. It now has a modern 28-inch Japanese barrel with a set of screw-in chokes, in addition to its ancient (ribless, which I like better) 26-inch one.

My project gun, the Sauer. It weighs 8½ pounds and has the tightest (and most perfectly equal) bores and chokes I've ever seen. It fits well. It's a little loose, though not "off the face"; that is, it's perfectly safe to shoot. I'd like to lengthen its forcing cones and take out some of the choke, perhaps even put in screw-chokes from Briley's of Houston so I can use it as a sit-down dove gun. Aesthetically, it's almost perfect — a bit of scroll, 32-inch barrels, a shallow pistol grip, and a splinter forend with an ebony tip. It needs a stock refinish, and currently bears an awful vented recoil pad with a white spacer. All in time.

Rifles. Roy is still working on the 7 x 57. It's gorgeous. I also have my father's old .30/.30, a pre-64 Model 94. I have fitted it with a peep sight, and otherwise left it alone. It kills deer if I get close enough.

Handguns. My pride and joy is a Smith & Wesson Classic Hunter in .44 magnum, a stainless steel model with a 6½-inch barrel. My only addition to the original was to replace the factory grips with smooth rosewood Skeeter Skelton custom stocks by Bearhug. They make shooting it far more pleasant. If I had to do it over again, I might go for an inch less barrel for comfort in carrying, but I like it pretty well.

For a .22, I have a utilitarian Ruger single-action with the 5½-inch barrel, with an extra .22 magnum cylinder, in blue. All in all, I might prefer a Bisley or a Smith, but with a trigger job and a nice leather cowboy-style holster by Bianchi, it does just fine.

I also own a small-frame .38 by Smith and a Chinese Colt .45 auto clone, but these are not really country guns.

Wants? One above all: an English game gun, in a light 12 or a standard 16. For romance's sake and my standards, I want it made in England. It should probably be a boxlock (not that I'd turn down a gift sidelock, but I've actually come to prefer the better boxlocks aesthetically.) More importantly: It should have 28-inch barrels, a high straight-hand stock of at least 14½ inches with a little cast-off, and weigh under 6¼ pounds (12) or a little under 6 (16).

I'd also like a good .22, a big bore double rifle (which I may never afford), and a large lever gun in .45/70 or .348. If I live long enough....

Good hunting.

Appendix III:

Recommended Reading

This is a minimum list.

Richard Akehurt: *Game Guns and Rifles* (Sportsman's Press, 1992). Reprint of the 1964 book. Great on English gun history.

Bob Brister: *Shotgunning, The Art and the Science* (Winchester Press, 1976). Bob Brister is the best technical gun writer in America. This book is indispensible. America's answer to Gough Thomas; or is it the other way around?

Major Sir Gerald Burrard: *The Modern Shotgun*, 3 vols. (second revised edition 1944; reprinted by Ashford Press Publishing, 1985). The best technical work on the English shotgun. The modestly priced new edition is available from Tideline.

Robert Churchill: (with Macdonald Hastings) *Robert Churchill's Game Shooting* (Countrysport, 1992). Reprint of the revised 1971 edition. Still the best book on how to shoot with the shotgun.

W.W. Greener: *The Gun and Its Development* (the 9th edition of 1910 is considered the best, and is available in an inexpensive modern reprint from Crown). A broader, more historical view than Burrard in one volume, that includes rifles.

Elmer Keith: Any and all.

Michael McIntosh: *A.H. Fox: `The Finest Gun in the World'* (Countrysport, 1992). The best book on an American classic.

Marco Nobili: *Fucili D'Autore: The Best Guns* (London Guns, Santa Barbara, CA, 1992). The text, in both Italian and English, contains some of the strangest translation this side of a Japanese appliance manual. But the pictures of world-class guns, and the information, are wonderful.

Jack O' Connor: Any and all.

Paxton Quigley: *Armed and Female.* The single best introduction to handguns for anyone, male or female.

Gough Thomas (G.T. Garwood): *Shotgun Shooting Facts* (Winchester, 1978), *Shotguns and Cartridges for Game and Clays* (A & C Black, 1975), *Gough Thomas's Gun Book* (A & C Black, 1969). This English engineer may be the world's best technical gun writer, if only because he has been around longer than Brister (who quotes him).

Don Zutz: *The Double Shotgun* (Winchester, 1978) and *The Double Shotgun*, Revised Expanded Edition (Winchester, 1985). You really need both volumes of this comprehensive account of fine doubles. No book has them all; together, these two come closest.

Appendix IV:

Glossary

ACTION — The primary operational part of any gun, consisting of the breech, bolt, receiver, feeding, and firing mechanism, both rifle and shotgun. In shotguns, the firing mechanisms consist of those for double-barreled guns, pump-action guns, and autoloading (sometimes incorrectly called "automatic") guns. In rifles, the feeding/firing mechanisms are: single-shot (of which the falling block is the finest example), bolt-action, lever-action, double (the same form as over-under and side-by-side shotguns), pump, and autoloader. In handguns, the feeding and firing mechanisms are single-action, double-action, or autoloading. ("Single-action" means the hammer must be manually cocked between shots; a "double-action" can be fired by pulling the trigger.)

ANSON & DEELEY— An action that makes up the huge proportion of boxlock shotguns, invented in 1875 by two Westley Richards gunsmiths.

BAR ACTION SIDELOCK — An action in which the firing mechanisms (locks) are arranged so that the mainspring is in front of the hammers. Considered stronger than the back action.

BACK ACTION SIDELOCK — The mainspring of the lock is behind the tumbler.

BARREL FLATS — The underside of the barrels of a double gun where the barrels meet the water table of the receiver. Often, important information such as proof marks and maximum loads are stamped here.

BEAVERTAIL FOREND — A forend type found primarily on shotguns that widens and thickens closer to the action. The primary use is to keep the forward hand away from hot barrels.

BEST GUN — A semi-subjective term indicating a certain quality shotgun, normally a London-made,* sidelock shotgun. The lure of the Best gun is that it is almost entirely made by hand to the customer's specifications, including stock fit, weight, balance, barrel length, engraving, etc. In short, the "best" shotgun human hands are capable of creating. Such guns are normally "game guns," those used for shooting upland game as opposed to waterfowl.

BESPOKE — A gun that is made to order, in every regard, for its owner: gauge, fit, weight, chambers, specific load, patterns, rib, wood, checkering, engraving, etc. This term is normally associated with England, "custom" being the term in America. A bespoke shotgun is very often a Best gun, although there are makers from Spain, Italy, and Birmingham in England who will produce a bespoke gun. The terminology gets a bit confusing, for a gun made to order is "bespoke," but if it is a Birmingham boxlock, it cannot be called a "Best" gun.

BORE — In a shotgun, "gauge"; but also the inside of the barrel in shotgun, rifle, or pistol (see "gauge").

* and possibly the product of two Scottish makers: Dickson and McKay Brown.

BUTT — The part of the stock that is held against the shoulder during firing, rifle or shotgun.

BITE — The under-locking lug mechanism consisting of the notches into which a bolt slides when a break-action gun is closed.

CALIBER — For rifles and handguns. Calibers are most often designated by the diameter of the bullet in inches, or (for Continental cartridges) in millimeters, such as .308 or 7mm. The .410 shotgun is a caliber, not a gauge.

CASE-HARDEN — A method of surface hardening the receiver of guns, especially shotguns, to make them more impervious to rust and corrosion. The technique involves heating the parts in a furnace while packed in organic (high in carbon) materials; bone meal is a common agent. The parts are then quenched in water, and the result is an uncommon color scheme that greatly adds to the beauty of a fine gun.

CAST — The distance a shotgun stock bends away from the face of a shooter. Cast allows the shooter to "face the shot," making it easy to pivot with the target. Picture a right-handed shooter, standing so that his hands are at his sides as he faces a stationary target. His eye and his shoulder pocket, where the stock will rest, are not lined up, vertically, with one another. A bend in the stock so that the eye lines up with the plane of the bores and the butt of the stock still meets his shoulder pocket necessitates a bend of the stock away from the shooter's face ("cast-off"). Left-handed shooters, and some right-handers, have the stock bent in the other direction ("cast-on").

CHAMBER — Where the shotgun shell, rifle or pistol cartridge is housed immediately prior to firing.

CHOKE — The amount of constriction in the end (normally about the last two inches) of a shotgun barrel. The degree of constriction determines the size of the pattern at 40 yards (see "pattern") and therefore the choke. Choke is not a designation of constriction, but is one of performance. Sometimes, very tight patterns can be achieved by very little constriction. Chokes can be adjusted to be made more open by judicious honing; however, putting choke back into a barrel or tightening it is nearly impossible to do satisfactorily. The standard choke gradients are: cylinder (no choke), skeet, improved cylinder, modified, improved modified, full, and (rarely) extra-full. Generally, Americans, besides shooting too much gun and too much shot, also use too much choke. Day in and day out, improved cylinder in a one-barreled gun or improved cylinder/modified (or improved modified) in a double prove satisfactory. Contrary to some lingering opinion, barrel length does not regulate choke; a 32-inch-barreled waterfowl gun with improved cylinder choke will shoot an improved cylinder pattern at 40 yards.

CROSSBOLT — A device used on many shotguns and most heavy double rifles that strengthens the mechanism that holds the gun closed under the stresses of firing. Most such bolts pass through an extension of the top rib and hold the breech down during recoil. Most shotguns of Germanic derivation have a crossbolt of some type.

DAMASCUS STEEL — A method of making gun barrel steel, popular in the days before modern (fluid) steels. A mixture of iron strips wrapped around a mandrel and hardened by fire and hammering to forage a one-piece unit. Such steel has a tell-tale swirled, brown pattern, regarded as very attractive by gun fanciers. Damascus steel, however, is subject to weak spots because of corrosion that can permeate the area between iron strips, and also because of the age of most Damascus guns. The only way to be sure that such a gun is safe is to shoot with modern (nitro) loads is to have the gun certified as such by the London or Birmingham Proof House. Since no proof house exists in the United States, Damascus guns are generally considered to be unsafe with modern loads no matter what their apparent condition.

DROP — A shotgun or rifle stock is angled down as it extends backward. The amount of this downward angle from the line of the bores is referred to as the "drop." Modern shotguns and rifles have little drop compared to guns of the last century because shooters today keep their heads down more than was the accepted style years ago.

ENGRAVING — The artisty on the exposed metal parts of a gun. Engraving cuts down on reflective glare, but its main function is decoration. The steel may be engraved with swirls and patterns, such as Purdey's famous rosette-and-scroll; with photo-realistic scenes, such as Italian banknote or "bulino" engraving; with precious metals such as gold, which can be inlaid into the metal's surface; or a combination of all of these. Today, on a Best grade gun, nearly 30% of the cost of the gun will be for the desired engraving, nearly twice as much as the cost for the stock carving, fitting, finishing, and checkering.

FENCES — The rounded sections of the standing breech at the ends of the barrels of a side-by-side double. Originally, they were higher and were used to keep burning powder away from the eyes of shooters of flintlock guns. Today, they aid in strengthening the standing breech against recoil.

FIT — Although most guns are made for a mythical "average" shooter, most people will shoot better with a gun, shotgun or rifle, that fits them. The measurements critical to fit are drop, length of pull, and cast. Gun stocks, especially shotguns stocks, can be altered by sanding, bending, cutting, or adding a recoil pad or wood. Most experienced shooters have all their stocks fitted the same. Experienced fitters, using try-guns, can give a novice a good fit, but the best fit comes from the experience of the shooter himself. Fit is something that changes with age. Most shooters, as they get older, require a bit more drop to compensate for joints that have grown less flexible.

FORCING CONE — the area from the chamber forward in a shotgun where the chamber (larger than the gauge) tapers down to the bore diameter of the gauge. If these forcing cones are tapered too quickly or acutely, the gun will be hard-recoiling and the patterns will be unsatisfactory.

FOREND — Sometimes "forearm" or "fore-end," it is the wood under the barrels of a shoulder gun that provides a platform for the leading, non-trigger, hand. Classic game guns have traditional slim "splinter" forends because the shooter should properly grasp the barrels at the end of the forend, with just the tip of the wood resting in the palm of his hand. The forend also houses the ejector mechanism in double shotguns.

GAME GUN — A gun built for upland shooting, most often a British designation for a gun that is (almost always) 12-gauge with splinter forend, straight grip, 28- to 30-inch barrels, double triggers, a weight of 6½ pounds or under, and intended to fire loads of one ounce of shot or a fraction more. Both sidelock and boxlock guns deserve the designation of game gun.

GAUGE — Shotguns are measured in gauges (except for .410, which is a caliber). Originally, the measurement came from the number of lead balls, each equal in size to the inside bore diameter of the gun, that it would take to equal one pound. For example, in a 12-gauge, the inside bore diameter is .729; the number of lead balls, each .729 in size, that it takes to equal one pound is 12. The smaller the bore diameter of the shotgun, the more balls it takes to equal one pound, therefore the higher the number — 20 balls each 615 diameter will equal one pound, therefore a gun with a bore diameter of .615 is a 20-gauge.

GRIP — Where the trigger hand grasps the wood of the stock (also "hand" or "wrist"). Straight, English-style grips have no curve, while the alternate forms are semi- or full pistol grips. Straight grips are found on classic game guns and are the preferred grip for a shotgun with two triggers because the hand can more easily slide from one trigger to the next along a straight grip.

HAMMER/HAMMERLESS — Referring to the visible or hidden hammers on a shotgun or, rarely, a handgun. All guns have hammers (tumblers); if they are internal, the gun is designated "hammerless." Nearly all shotguns made today are hammerless, the exception being some high-grade Italian guns.

HAND — British designation for the grip.

LOCK — The firing mechanism of the gun, normally consisting of the hammers, sears, firing pins, and associated springs and hardware.

MAGNUM — A designation indicating more power in a given load — shotgun, rifle, or handgun. In rifles and handguns, this is accomplished by more propellant (powder) in the cartridge; in a shotgun, more shot and correspondingly more powder. The advantages of rifle and pistol magnum cartridges are much more readily apparent to their respective users than are the advantages to shotgunners of magnum shotshells.

OFF THE FACE — A British term that refers to wear in the action, creating a gap between the barrels and the standing breech.

PATTERN — The shot dispersal of a shotgun, normally recorded as the percentage of the shot (pellets) inside a 30-inch circle at 40 yards (25 yards for a .410). Patterns are a function of the choke in the shotgun barrel and the load; hard shot — deforming less — flies truer toward the mark, stays in the pattern, and therefore tends to make the pattern tighter.

PROOF — The British and European method by which the government certifies guns of all types to be safe for use. This is accomplished by sending the gun to a government proof house where it is fired with very heavy overload charges — "proof loads." If the gun survives, it is certified by marks on the barrel flats of the gun. America has no proof house, so for the sake of ensuring safety, American gunmakers have traditionally overbuilt their shotguns. Proof houses, certifying a gun safe for a given load, removes the liability risk from the maker. This allows European gunmakers to trim away the last few ounces of wood and steel to make the lightest shotgun that is also certified safe.

PULL — The length of the stock from the trigger, or the front trigger in a double-trigger gun, to the middle of the butt of the stock.

American standard is about 14½ inches. English stock fitters normally fit shooters sensibly longer than this, claiming the shooter "stays with the gun" a bit better with a longer stock. This may be the easiest measurement for the shooter to fit to himself. If, even when mounted properly, the stock hangs up in his clothing, it is too long; if he bangs his nose with his thumb during recoil, it's too short.

RIB — the portion of the barrel that runs along the top. In over-unders and single-barreled guns, it is used as a sighting aid and, in the case of a ventilated rib, for heat dispersal. In a side-by-side double, the ribs also serve to hold the barrels together. Most side-by-side doubles have a top and bottom rib. The top rib of such guns can be dead level, elevated and tapering (Churchill rib), or dropping below the plane of the barrels until it rises to meet the muzzle (swamped rib).

SIDE CLIPS — Small extensions on the side of the fences designed to keep the barrels from twisting during recoil.

SIDELOCK — A type of shotgun and double rifle action in which the lock (firing) mechanism is housed behind lockplates and is separate from the main housing of the receiver, as in a boxlock action. Such guns present a great area for engraving, and some say sidelock trigger pulls can be made more uniform. Sidelock guns are often fractionally heavier than their boxlock counterparts and also weaker through the stock because of the amount of wood that has to be removed to inlet the locks.

SIDE-PLATE — Really a boxlock action made to look like a sidelock gun for beauty's sake by using false plates called side-plates.

SNAP CAPS — Dummy cartridges, most often of nickel-plated brass, used to cushion firing pins so the gun can be dry-fired to test trigger pulls and for practice.

SPINDLE — The connection between the top lever and the mechanism that slides the bolts back on a double gun. The Scott spindle is the basis for all such arrangements.

STANDING BREECH — The section of the receiver of a double shotgun housing the firing pins.

WATER TABLE — The flats of the receiver of a double shotgun.

Parts of a Boxlock Double Gun

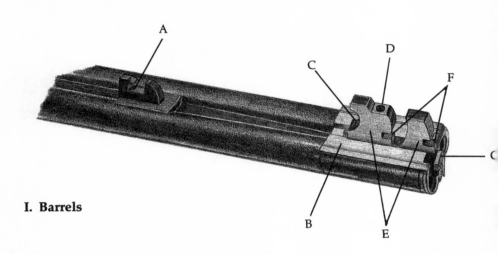

I. Barrels

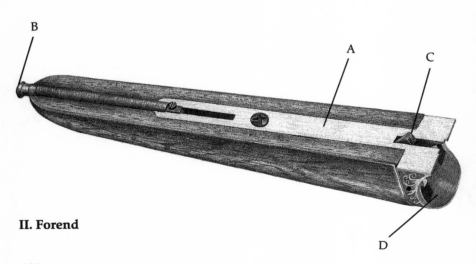

II. Forend

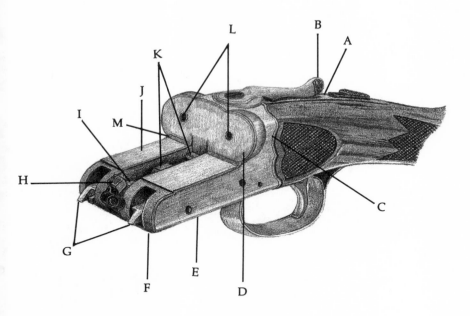

III. Action Body

I. Barrels
A—Forend lub; B—Barrel flats; C—Hook (mates with the hingepin); D—Ejector retaining screw; E—Lumps; F—Bites; G—Ejectors

II. Forend
A—Forend iron; B—Forend latch; C—Ejector hammers; D—Ejector sears

III. Action Body
A—Top tang; B—Top lever; C—Fences; D—Standing breech; E—Action bar; F—Knuckle; G—Cocking levers; H—Extractor toe; I—Hinge-pin; J—Water table; K—bolts; L—Firing pins; M—Break-off

Good Guns Again

was

edited by Steve Smith

and

designed by Ganay Johnson.